Plain Bread

Plain Bread

BEN KINCHLOW

with Bob Slosser

WORD BOOKS
PUBLISHER
WACO, TEXAS

A DIVISION OF
WORD, INCORPORATED

Plain Bread

Copyright © 1985 by Word, Incorporated

Library of Congress Cataloging in Publication Data

Kinchlow, Ben, 1936–
  Plain bread.

  1. Kinchlow, Ben, 1936–   . 2. Evangelists—United
States—Biography. I. Slosser, Bob. II. Title.
BV3785.K56A35 1985   269′.2′0924 [B]   85–2295
ISBN 0–8499–0461–7

Printed in the United States of America

For
Mom, Dad, and *Junior;*
Vivian, Nigel, Levi, and *Sean;*
and *John*

Contents

Preface

As you read this book, please check out the Scripture refer-
ences. I hope you'll take time to look them up in a Bible. I
happen to have quoted from the King James Version throughout this project, but that's no big deal. Use any translation,
especially if you're not comfortable with the KJV. Some marvelous translations have come along in recent years and
they're often easier reading, providing greater insight. So take
advantage of them as you read this story, for the Word of
God is what's really important.

Some of you may wonder why I chose to call this book
Plain Bread. Well, "plain bread" is just that—simple, plain
grub. It's real. It's not fancy. It's down to earth—even homely.
In this case, it's sometimes downright ugly. I think you will
understand.

My collaborator, Bob Slosser, and I owe a debt of gratitude
to a number of people for their help with this manuscript.
We're thankful for all the patient and helpful people at Word,
especially "Big" Ernie Owen and Al Bryant, and we deeply
appreciate the self-sacrificing labors of Ruth Ann Arnold and
Susan Norman of Virginia Beach, Virginia.

BEN KINCHLOW
February 1, 1985

Prologue

I pulled off the street into the long, U-shaped parking lot. Barracks were on both sides. His was on the left. The buildings in this part of Shaw Air Force Base were better than those at a lot of other bases—tan, concrete block, two-story, long, and well kept. I remember the lawns, deep green and closely trimmed, and the neat sidewalks leading right up to the sides of the buildings.

GI's were returning from lunch in considerable numbers, yet everything had an eerie quietness to me; the light-blue sky seemed far away.

I got out of the car slowly, deliberately. My right hand felt the cold metal of the gun in my pocket. It was a .25 automatic, black—they called it blue—and the clip was in place, loaded with eight shells.

I walked easily up the sidewalk. I was perfectly calm. No pounding heart, no dry mouth, no quivering hand. I counted the steps leading to the barracks door—four. *So this is what it's like,* I thought. I almost smiled. *Cold-blooded murder. It means just what it says. I'm perfectly cool.*

I went into the building, stepping into a foyer. The CQ— the one in charge of quarters—was behind a table over to the right. He looked up.

"Can you tell me where Smith's room is—O. C. Smith's?" I asked.

He pointed across the room toward the hall. "It's right over there across the hall."

The CQ went back to his papers. I walked to the hall and was almost out of his sight, but not quite. I looked at the door. It was medium brown, very plain. I stared at it as I approached. I had no fear, no hesitancy, in those few seconds. I did not think about prison or the electric chair. I did not think about my children and the certainty that they would grow up without a father. I did not think about my parents. None of those things was a deterrent, despite what the sociologists might argue. I was going to kill this man. That's all.

I flipped the safety off the gun with my thumb and eased my hand around the grip. I reached toward the door with my left hand. One-two-three-four-five, I knocked. Then I stepped back. My finger curled around the trigger. I would start shooting the second the door opened. I had no idea what he looked like, but I was going to blow away the man who opened that door. I would let him have five shots. I would then follow him into the room and pump the other three slugs into him for good measure. I could see him bleeding. My heartbeat began to pick up the pace.

No sounds came. I reached forward again. Knock-knock, pause, knock-knock. I stepped back. I waited. Silence. Fifteen seconds passed. Then I knocked once more. No answer.

With the gun still ready to fire, I turned and walked back to the CQ. "Where's Smith?" I asked. "I thought he was here."

The airman reached for the log in front of him. A red line was drawn through a name. "Oh, sorry," he mumbled. "See, he's gone on TDY. He left today."

Temporary duty? On the day I arrived? I couldn't believe it. I gave the CQ a blank look and muttered something like, "Oh, I see. Well, I'll have to catch him later. Thanks."

I walked out, forcing the safety back into place on the automatic. I got into the car and drove away, headed toward our house.

"I'll get Vivian," I said half-aloud. "I'll go back and kill her." I was almost oblivious to my surroundings, steering the car by instinct. "I'll kill her, and get him later."

Muddy, disconnected thoughts skipped through my mind. *I hate her . . . No, I love her . . . I should have gone after him yesterday . . . The kids . . . Where can I go? It's all so messed up . . . I'll go home to Uvalde. . . .*

By the time I reached our house, I knew I could not kill Vivian. I wanted to hurt her, yes, but I could not kill her. As I stopped in front of the house, I shoved the gun into the glove compartment, unwilling to take it inside, now afraid of what I might do with it.

"I'm taking the boys," I said aloud to myself. "I'll take them to Texas and leave them."

With the decision came resolve. I walked into the house and calmly called for Nigel and Levi. "Come on. You're going with me."

Vivian came into the room. "What are you doing? Where are you going? Where are you taking my boys?" She was moving toward hysteria. I'm certain she knew my desperation.

"I'm leaving, and I'm taking them," I said flatly.

"You're not taking my boys!"

I stopped in the middle of the room, and I stared at her. Murder was in my eyes, and they fixed on hers. I fear that if she had said or done anything more, I would have seriously harmed her—perhaps worse.

She apparently could see that in my eyes. I was calm and cool, but I probably was insane at the moment. She looked at me, but said nothing. Tears formed in her eyes.

After a second or so of hard staring—it seemed like minutes—I said, "Okay, boys, let's go."

"Where are we going, Daddy?" It was Nigel.

"Just get in the car," I said.

The two of them started out, and Vivian began to cry. She followed us to the small front porch and stood there crying as I started across the yard. "Let's talk," she said. "Don't go! Let's talk."

I said nothing. Unhurriedly I got into the car, pulled the door shut, started the engine, and drove off—all without looking at her. Two little boys huddled together, tiny and confused, crying.

Plain Bread

1

What's with This Guy?

I KNEW I WAS OUT OF CONTROL. But it was too late; I couldn't stop. I pounded the table once and the dishes jumped. There was a definite possibility that I would smash the entire table, beautifully laid for dinner for six. In my mind the whole scene dissolved into a confusion of shattered china, flying silverware, torn tablecloth, chicken and mashed potatoes—madness.

I knew I should get a grip on myself, but the control I usually managed to keep on my rage had slipped. Somehow I wasn't screaming; my voice seemed to be the only part of me that wasn't boiling. But I wasn't sure that would last. I could feel the cords in my neck bulging, and my facial muscles pulling at the corners of my mouth. I was certain the veins were standing out on my forehead, and I could feel the sweat collecting all over my face. My chest and back were starting to get wet.

I looked straight into John Corcoran's face opposite me. "What we have to do is turn these young black street gangs into murderous bands of real guerrilla fighters—train them, teach them how to fight, how to survive off the land—and set them loose in the countryside of Mississippi and Alabama and Georgia and let them wipe out those rednecks. . . ."

All the real or imagined slights of my past rushed pell-mell into my memory, increasing my fury. "The land of the free and the home of the brave? Liberty and justice for all? Ha! For the white folks, that is." I stretched my arms wide and gripped the edge of the table, giving it a short, violent shake. The dishes rattled once more.

My wife, Vivian, stared into her plate and picked slowly, without purpose, at the chicken breast on it. Her fork never came to her mouth. She was embarrassed to the point of tears. I had acted this way with her many times in the last two years and she had grown to expect these outbursts. But why was I abusing these gentle, kindly people who had invited us into the warmth of their home?

And my mother—the spiritual backbone of all the Kinch-lows—was clearly horrified. I knew she was frantic inside, wishing, hoping, praying desperately that I'd run out or shut up. This was no way for good, Christian people to act with gracious hosts—white people, especially—who had opened their home so fully to one of Uvalde's dozen or more black families. What had happened to the polite boy who had always said "Yes ma'am" and "No sir"; the boy she had carefully nurtured during the hazardous years of the forties and fifties?

Here he was—spouting rage, pouring out a ferocious blend of Malcolm X, Middle East Marxism, and street-wise Ben Kinchlow, thirty-two-year-old Air Force veteran, world traveler, and recent big-man-on-campus: The black man must seize power, real power, control of big money, big business, big clout. This would doubtless mean physical force—violence. "The Man" wasn't just going to roll over and play dead, but the violence would be smart violence, with prepared, trained, equipped revolutionaries poised for strategic action. The white man owed the black man for one hundred years of slavery and discrimination—the American Constitution's "certain inalienable rights" proved that—and if the white man wasn't going to pay up, then a second American Revolution had to come.

I spouted my rage right across the table to probably the only real friend I had at that rocky point in my life, a quiet, decent man. He was a minister of the gospel, and I was suspicious of that, but as a judo expert he had joined right in with me—a karate specialist—to teach a self-defense class at college, and we had been spending a lot of time together. Yet I was boiling him in my venom. Why?

His wife, Joy, also a student, was getting the fallout, though, and she too picked nervously at her plate. And my dad—I wouldn't even look at him. But I felt his frozen stare from the side. The muscles of his face were locked into place. What had happened to his oldest boy, the one he had worked so hard to provide for?

The problem was simple: These people did not understand. Safe in their little Texas womb, they hadn't run headlong into that big dirty world out there. Oh, Vivian, being from the north, had some understanding, but not much. She was a woman. And that was different. Black women were never perceived as a threat. They cooked the white man's meals, took care of the sick, raised his children, had his babies. They were not dangerous. It was the male—the buck—who was the object of fear and rage. "Let them in the schools," the argument went, "and they'll be in our beds." No one seemed to notice that they, the whites, were already in ours.

No, the people at this cozy little dinner party hadn't stood in a Virginia department store alongside a little son, just recently potty-trained, as a minimum-wage clerk with a superior attitude told him he couldn't use their restrooms. They hadn't been humiliated in an Air Force barbershop, having to walk through the white man's shop all the way to the little cubbyhole in back for "coloreds." They hadn't stood proud and tall in a United States military uniform and then been forced to the rear of a Louisiana bus. No, and they hadn't experienced the freedom of the blacks in many Middle Eastern countries, felt pride in seeing men with dark skins and kinky hair rise to the top of their professions and even into national and international prominence in positions of leadership.

No, they didn't understand. But I did. And I also knew what it was like to feel a family torn and twisted and destroyed by the strains and frustrations and fears that somehow seemed to penetrate much of black America. I knew about male frustration and pent-up anger. I knew firsthand about drunkenness, infidelity, crime, abortion, selfishness, hate. I had been there, I *was* there, I had done it all—I was doing it at the time.

Yes, I understood, and at that moment I was out of control. At that moment, maybe I didn't care. Let it happen!

I clenched my teeth and fists in a final spasm of anger and, breathing heavily, stared hard across the table into the face of Corcoran, this nondescript, sandy-haired young preacher with the long nose. He looked into my eyes. I wanted him to feel my hatred, my contempt, my anger, my pain. His face was absolutely expressionless, no frown, no grimace—only slightly red from embarrassment. He was looking, not at me, but inside me.

Several seconds went by, and I found my rage subsiding, like a storm that had blown itself out. The clock ticked loud in the silence. Suddenly it dawned on me. John was crying. He wasn't making any sound or screwing his face up like a little kid. His eyes had filled up, and tears were running down his cheeks.

For a flash of a second, I was even more enraged. *The honky's upset because I'm ruining his little party,* I thought. *I really ought to walk out of here.* But then I stopped, because I knew—somehow I knew—he wasn't crying out of embarrassment or anger. He didn't care about what the others thought. Then in sudden awareness, I knew something else for certain. John Corcoran cared about me. He was weeping because he cared. He was hurt because I was hurting. I had never dreamed anyone could care this much about another human being outside his own family, certainly not about me and my frustration, my bitterness, my anger, the things that were eating me alive from the inside like acid. That unusual little guy—a white guy—loved me.

* * *

After an uneasy pause, we went back to eating, and attempted strained conversation about ordinary things like college, our children, gossip around Uvalde, and the self-defense class John and I taught. In a few short minutes we were able to laugh a little, and we almost enjoyed the fine dinner Joy Corcoran had prepared. She had put out her best for us. Still the effect of my outburst hung sullenly like a cloud after a storm over the rest of the evening.

On the way home I spoke very little. I kept thinking about John and his tears. What was that all about? Grown men don't cry over other grown men. John Corcoran was the squarest, straightest, emotionally strongest person I'd known. His tears were clean, totally healthy. There was nothing weird about John Corcoran—except that he loved me. Words formed in my mind, and I said them aloud under my breath.

"How can anybody love me? *I* don't even love me! I have to find out what makes this guy tick."

* * *

It was a time of lurching change in America and the world, the sixties. My fury, which more often than not sprang from a lifetime of quiet, often imperceptible insecurity, was not unique. Millions of men, women, and children shared it with me. I expressed it differently from many others because in many ways I suppose I felt I was different—people said I was more sophisticated, more controlled, more articulate. And I was selfish. I wanted to break out for no other reason than myself. Sure, I thought about black people and their condition. I thought about injustice on a wide scale. But Ben Kinchlow was at the center of those thoughts. What was good for blacks was good—if it was good for Ben Kinchlow.

I was moving pretty much along the mainstream of black nationalism. I felt that Malcolm X, who had stirred the hearts and minds of millions, made the most sense. If we were to escape oppression, we must be smart and fearless. And, somewhat contrary to Malcolm's speeches in his later days, I was certain there would be times for violence—yes, bloodshed. But the main thing was to move into power and control, before the revolution if possible—but to gain the upper hand whatever the cost.

Yet, lurking like a specter over and around it all was a creeping, smothering insecurity. I talked big, and often. I had learned I could move audiences on occasion. But my inner confidence did not match the outer facade. I often bit my fingernails to the quick and beyond.

This, and many other strains on my life—also typical of those churning times among blacks and whites alike—was tearing my family apart, just as it was doing to millions of other families. My relationships could not stand up under such stress and frustration. I knew that if something didn't happen quickly, Vivian and I would be divorced and our children would become statistics. My mother and father would be heartbroken.

It was a time of national, even international upheaval, and it was destroying individuals at a frantic pace. I personally was caught in a maelstrom of immorality. I was rotten to the core in some areas, and no high-sounding talk of "black politics" could erase that.

Was there any prospect for lasting peace on both the world scale and at the personal level? Was all this *really* life? Was this wrenching and tearing inevitable? Was that the "way it is"? Could men and women—black, white, brown, yellow— ever shed their deep-seated fears and hatred, their prejudice?

On that night in 1969, the night John Corcoran saw the real Ben Kinchlow and cried, the prospects did not look good.

2

Childhood

I TURNED MY HEAD ON THE PILLOW ever so slightly so I could see better. I didn't want them to know I was still awake. But I was fascinated. First, the red glow was very soft and dim; then all of a sudden it got really big and bright. It looked as though it would explode. Then it grew dim again. All the while it glided silently through the air. It was close by, but simultaneously as far away as the summer stars, as I fought manfully against sleep.

I was ten years old, and the heat was heavy in southwestern Texas. Our screened-in porch made sleep possible, even with just the slightest breeze, during those summer months. I could remember when we had not had the porch across the back of our house, and sleeping on those sultry nights had been out of the question. This was like heaven. With it, our little house seemed twice as big.

But that red glow in the dark night was special. The memory of it flits in and out of my mind to this day. It just hung in space. Actually it wasn't very mysterious at all. My dad— "Daddy" in those growing-up years—seemed always to smoke his last cigarette of the long, hard day out there in the quiet darkness before going to bed. And the recurring memory of my childhood is of that floating red glow and the comfort and security of those few minutes before sleep swallowed me.

It is a memory of "everything's okay; Daddy and Mama are here; there's nothing to be afraid of."

That's the way it was with Daddy. In those early days he got up around four o'clock, long before I was awake, and most times I would be in bed by the time he got home, or headed in that direction. I saw very little of him. But even when he wasn't present, he was felt. He brought strength, and enthusiasm, and security. He *was* that red glow.

Daddy worked hard. During my early years he worked seven days a week on a ranch and later for a dairy farm twelve miles from home. He either walked or rode a bicycle to and from his work. He would return after all the chores were completed following the milking each evening. He maintained that grinding regimen day after day, year after year, but his optimistic good nature never waned.

Later on, when he began to work at a creamery in town, he got Sundays off. I saw him a bit more, but not a lot, because he was a baseball player, one of the best in town. He played at least one game, often a doubleheader, each Sunday. And he thrived on it. I'm sure he could have made the big leagues had those things been possible for blacks at that time. But he settled for Sundays, working like a dog all week and then pouring himself out totally on the baseball field on his day of rest. He was a fabulous player, expert at almost any position, especially catcher, and outstanding in center field or at first base.

I can remember the scene well. It's Sunday. Mama and Daddy sleep an extra hour or two and then things begin to bustle. Daddy's laughing and bending over and pulling on his socks. Mama's dressing for church. I'm just hanging around, watching. Then I pick my spot. "Daddy, can I go with you to the game today?"

His smile eases ever so slightly, he glances right at me, and solemnly says, "You go along to church, Ben." The big smile flashes again. "You see me play enough."

And that was that. You didn't argue on the subject of church. Daddy believed in church for me and Mama. He didn't go, but Mama and I did. However, there were the doubleheaders. And, although a lot of black people spent almost all of Sunday in church—at least it seemed like it to me—I was allowed to go with Daddy to some of the afternoon games. And how I relished those days when the team played over in Crystal City thirty-seven miles away and I could tag along.

The thing about Daddy that was so appealing was simple: he was alive. He was strong. Yet he was always laughing—a quick, full-blown, hearty laugh. He was not a big man; in fact, he was a shade shorter than my mother. But he was the most alive man I remember from my childhood. He made other men seem grim and pale by comparison.

Like that cigarette on hot, oppressive evenings, he glowed in the darkness, sometimes red hot, sometimes dimmer, but always glowing and moving.

* * *

Mama was one of those ladies who simply refused to be defeated by anything. She was an overcomer in every sense of the word—persistent, patient, and proud. Hard work and determination were the key ingredients in her life.

My earliest remembrances are of her rushing off to church, rushing off to teach school, rushing off to attend summer school, rushing off to help somebody who was sick, including my grandfather who had moved in with us when his health failed. It seemed to my little self-centered mind that Mama was always rushing off to help somebody, and I wasn't sure I liked it.

Like Daddy, Mama laughed a lot. She was animated, enthusiastic. But she could be stern, too; in fact, tough. I guess that was the schoolteacher in her. But it was more than that. It was the determination, the refusal to be defeated by the harshness of life. And standing her ground wasn't enough. She insisted on gaining ground and moving forward, even if it were only a quarter of an inch at a time. Even when a nerve condition and a doctor's mistake combined to cause almost total blindness, she moved on and overcame that, too.

With hindsight, I believe this quality grew out of her relationship with God. She believed God. She believed He was real, present, listening. And she talked to Him, in a rather ordinary, intimate, easy-going way. I can see her moving quickly about our little kitchen, the house's all-purpose room, working hard as always, cooking, scrubbing, ironing, and the words dropped naturally from her lips—"Precious Lord . . . Blessed Jesus . . . Lord, have mercy. . . ." The words were always before me, part of my life, yet they had little meaning to me.

But Mama's strength was real. She made things happen. I had no sense of matriarchy in my childhood—Daddy was the boss—but Mama was more prominent in my life those first years. When I close my eyes tight, I can see her plainly—a tall, medium-brown-skinned lady who wore her hair like the Indian stereotype, parted down the middle and pulled straight down on each side. That, of course, heightened her serious, stern moments.

Mama's dominance in my early life was also attributable to her career. She indeed was my teacher, not only at home but in school.

Uvalde, a collection of roughly 10,000 people in those days, was not one of the hotbeds of racial prejudice in America. In all honesty, our little southwestern Texas town probably had less discrimination than many communities its size because it contained only a dozen or so black families at that time, and this kept the social and economic friction low.

The basis for most friction is economic competition. Remove those people in a community who will work for less money, either because of status or desire, and you ease friction. The Chinese coolie, the Mexican peasant, the Irish or Italian immigrant, have all been discriminated against for economic reasons.

But there was segregation. I went to one of the South's "separate but equal" schools. To us, the phrase meant we got the hand-me-downs. When the white schools were ready to discard their softball or basketball equipment they passed it on to us. When our playground—a field behind the school—needed basketball goals, Dad and some other black men in the neighborhood got some big cedar posts and sunk them into the ground, and we had backboards.

That was the way it was, and my recollection is that it was no big problem as far as the kids were concerned. We had a school, and we seemed to have what we needed. We suspected the white schools were better, but I guess since we didn't know for sure, we didn't worry about it.

Our school was Nicolas Street School—that was what we called it, and if it ever had any other name, I don't remember it. It had two rooms, one for the first through fourth grades and one for the fifth, sixth, seventh, and eighth. The big gas stove that heated the building in the cold winters stands out in my mind. It was one of those seemingly insignificant "security blankets" that are scattered through everyone's childhood memories. The two rooms of the building were separated by a sliding partition. Each had one teacher, handling four grades. My mother was one of the teachers; she was also the principal.

There were twenty-five to thirty of us in the school, eight in my class, and I am convinced to this day that my mother was tougher on me than on any of the others. I'm sure the issue was favoritism, and she seemed to bend over backward to avoid any hint of it, expecting more of me than the other students. If I did something right—and I was no dummy—I didn't receive an A-plus. It was an A-minus. She never let me be the best; somehow there was always a little minus somewhere. And I had to toe the line in conduct, too. One little thing and she was all over me. I was "The Teacher's Kid," but there was no room for scandal about "Teacher's Pet."

I'm vaguely aware that this left a mark on me. I felt that I was probably more knowledgeable than my fellow students because I was a born reader. I read everything I could find— geography books, history books, magazines, and oh, yes, comic books when I could get my hands on them. I read them all. My favorites were the hand-me-down *National Geographics*. I devoured them, pictures and all. My always active imagination would carry me almost bodily to the four corners of the earth.

My interests ranged wide, but since Mama would never let me excel, at least in front of others, I may have picked up on a falsehood: I was somehow never quite good enough and people really didn't like me very much.

Nonetheless, I learned at Nicolas Street. As far as I was concerned, it was a good school. All my playmates and friends were there—even my own mother—and it was close to home.

All I had to do was step out the door, cut across a big grain field, and I was at school. I most likely would have been unhappy if I had to travel across town to some all-white, faraway facility. It would have made no sense to any of us.

Sure, we were segregated, but we didn't see it as segregation. So were the Mexicans, at least in elementary school, and they were more numerous in Uvalde than blacks. They went to West Main and West Garden Schools. In fact, they probably suffered more from racial discrimination than the blacks in our town, simply because their numbers heightened competition for jobs and they would work for less. But kids don't dwell on the idea of segregation and discrimination. We liked our school and we didn't care about much beyond our own neighborhood, which was not segregated.

There were only three or four black families in our immediate neighborhood. Miss Mariah, a black lady who made incredible butter cookies, lived right beside us. The Gaffords who lived on the other side of us were our cousins, and "Boob" and Alma Kinchlow, more relatives, lived up the street. Later on, the Moores moved close by. But the Marcos Hills lived two doors up from us, and they were Mexican, and there was a white family up the road. Domingo, a Mexican, lived behind Miss Mariah, and the Simon Flores family, Mexicans, lived on the corner. And there was Henry Rosenthal, who was Jewish. We assumed Henry was wealthy because he owned the biggest house in our neighborhood and drove a brand new truck.

So we were a mixture of everything—black, white, Mexican, Jewish. We didn't dwell on it. Nobody thought much about it, I'm sure. We played together, ate together, fought together—did everything together except go to school, and school wasn't for fun anyway.

The kids at Nicolas Street didn't give a lot of thought to poverty. Sure, our family was poor, but so it seemed was everyone else in the neighborhood. Poverty didn't exist for us. Our clothes may have been a bit raggedy, patched, or threadbare (mine were almost always too short), but we were all that way. And we were clean.

Furthermore, we seemed to have enough to eat. We all

took leftovers to school until hot lunches came along, but there was nothing strange about that. We were in it together. I remember occasional apples. Fruit was scarce and expensive, so when someone would finish an apple, we'd take "dibs" on the core. It sounds strange in today's affluence, but there didn't seem to be anything strange about it at that time. No one felt superior or inferior. Anyway, apple cores aren't all that bad.

Another factor was important in the lives of the little band at Nicolas Street School situated on the west side of town almost at the city limits. Throughout the black community there was a strong sense of moral concern among the responsible adults. Black kids were not allowed to get away with anything that was deemed improper—"not right," as they said. Almost every adult took it upon himself to be responsible for every black child in the community. If an adult saw a child doing something wrong, he'd correct him, to the point of giving a spanking if needed, and send the child home with a note to the parents. In most cases, the parents would add their own spanking, and the child learned to behave. It was genuine community responsibility, and the grown-ups seemed to have eyes in the backs of their heads.

*   *   *

For my first fourteen years, the center of life was our old clapboard house, unpainted, weathered and grayish, brightened by zinnias Mama planted. Struggling against the weather and other odds, they added little splashes of color to our house at the corner of Geraldine and Old Carrizo Road, two unpaved, dusty roads that crossed near the edge of town. It was a fine house as far as I was concerned—big then, small in retrospect—a fine house in a fine, sparsely populated, poor, happy, and peaceful neighborhood. And we were a fine family—my dad, my mom, and I, joined by my brother, Harvey Junior, when I was thirteen.

The hub of activity was the same as for most poor families of that era—the kitchen. The screened porch where we slept in the hot summers wonderfully expanded our private world. We had added it to the house just off the kitchen at the same time we installed indoor plumbing. Unless you've been without it, you can't really appreciate the thrill of flushing a commode inside your own house. I must have flushed it a thousand times just to hear that water rushing off to China or somewhere.

The big gas stove stood as the centerpiece of the kitchen, imprinted on my mind for its purposes other than cooking good food; it was a key element in our family routine. We took our baths in a big metal washtub placed right between the stove and the kitchen table, opening the oven door to warm and dry ourselves. I can remember standing there, long, skinny, naked, shivering like a plucked chicken until the waves of heat from that big old stove finally engulfed me and brought the warm, secure, cocoon feeling that survives every happy childhood for years.

The kitchen memories are also filled with Mama's marvelous cooking, turning ordinary, poor folks' poverty-marked groceries into culinary delights. But those worn, plain walls with their little cabinets and one or two old pictures witnessed more than cooking and kitchen work. They heard school lessons, parental lectures, bits and pieces of sacred singing, a mother's prayers, a hurt child's wailing, a father's reassurance. They heard the grunts and groans, the melodies and the miseries of a black family's minutes and days, months, and years—its real life, plain bread.

We always ate our meals off the table in the kitchen, and next to the kitchen was an average size room that we used as a bedroom when I was very young. And when my mother's father lost his health, he moved in with us and that was his room. It became known as the middle bedroom.

That room led to the living room in the front of the house, which opened onto our wide (from a child's point of view), grass-covered front yard. To the side of the living room, running along the front of the house, was my mother and father's bedroom. It was sort of the inner sanctum, and although it was in the front part of the house, to us it was the back bedroom.

Behind the house, between the new screened porch and the old outhouse several yards away was the chicken coop and little house where the chickens roosted at night. Outside the chicken house were two rows of boxes in which the chickens, in a procedure that baffled me, continually laid their eggs. Those cackling creatures were an integral part of the Kinchlows' daily routine—feeding, laying, messing, and gently clucking in the quiet hours of the day.

Also central to our home's profile were five large pecan trees, two in front, two on the side, and one toward the back. They dominated our L-shaped yard, which was covered with a thick carpet of grass in the front and along the front half of the side yard. Smack in the middle of the front yard was a hydrant, where we drank icy cold water on steaming Texas summer days. We'd drink till our stomachs ached.

To the distress of my mother, but happily for the kids in the neighborhood, the grass never in all those years took root in the rear half of our side yard. It was merely good clean dirt, just what we needed, and that was our playground. It was the site of hour upon hour of lived-out fantasy. We always imagined ourselves to be richer than Henry Rosenthal, the fellow with the big house and the new truck. We created huge ranches in the dirt, making buildings of every shape out of penny matches and string, then using the boxes to make barns and houses. We turned empty thread spools into cars. Outbursts of delight followed hours of deep concentration as we built our masterpieces.

The main players in all of this were the Four Musketeers—myself and three cousins who lived next door. There was Son, whose real name was Myrick; McGee, whose real name was McVay, and Kitsy, their sister and the only girl in the group. We played together, fought together, cried together, slept together, and ate together, closer by far than most brothers and sisters.

Their house stood just a few feet beyond our little playground and it too was bounded on the front and side by a thick carpet of green grass. A small vegetable garden, tended by my Uncle Kiddo, held forth along the side toward the back. And between the chickens in our backyard and Uncle Kiddo's garden, we enjoyed a good supply of fresh food. Daddy brought home plenty of fresh milk from the dairy to go along with the fried chicken and fresh vegetables.

Perhaps the most amazing feature to my child's mind in the days before we got our indoor plumbing was Uncle Kiddo's outdoor shower. Its main component was a big barrel that my uncle had suspended in the air on a makeshift frame. When the weather cooperated, rainwater collected in the barrel and was heated by the sun. Otherwise, we used a water hose to fill the barrel. While standing in the little enclosure under it, you could pull a cord and down would come the water through holes drilled in the bottom of the barrel. What a treat!

Miss Mariah lived on the other side, separated from us by an empty lot that was perfect for games of hide and seek and all-out battles between young cowboys and Indians. And then, for bigger purposes, there was the huge field across the street from our house. During the growing seasons, it bore maize, but the rest of the time it stood big and empty, suitable for everything from football on up. It was there that I saw my first airplane up close when one of the oldtime barnstormers set his craft down, quickly gathering a wide-eyed, openmouthed gang of raggedy kids.

* * *

On Saturdays—every second or third one—there were the "peelies." They were a significant part in the cycle of youthful life for three of Uvalde's Four Musketeers. My uncle—my mother's younger brother and the father of Son, McGee, and Kitsy—would round us three boys up, place a single chair in our midst, and cut our hair. It was a monthly outdoor ritual. I never could figure out why Kitsy escaped. She had hair, too, but no one seemed to notice.

Uncle Kiddo would plop us down in the chair, get a brutal finger lock on our heads, and with a pair of old hand clippers proceed to "peel" our heads. And I mean *peel*. He didn't leave a strand anywhere. Our heads were naked when he finished with us.

I remember that I always seemed to be last. I'm not sure why, but it may have been that Uncle figured he'd let his own boys undergo the torture first. Actually it was not painful in most respects, but by the time he got to me, number three, the clippers felt blistering hot. I can remember wanting to twist out of his grip and run, they were so hot.

Even with close family ties and an adequate supply of the things we really needed, I began experiencing too many doubts about my worth. It seemed to me that I never fully measured up, though I knew I was smart and well-intentioned. Maybe something was wrong with me. "Why am I always last?" I pondered. "Why doesn't Mama ever praise me in front of other people?" I was struggling with self-centered insecurity, even at that tender stage of ten, eleven, and twelve, but it was real.

Oddly, I don't believe racial prejudice was a factor in this inferiority complex beginning to show traces within me. If it was, I was not aware of it. I truly do not believe I thought of discrimination in those early years. Perhaps it was there in my subconscious mind, but I'm not sure.

I do remember, without any recollection of emotion, a time when my mother and I were coming out of the movies, and a white man who was passing by put his hand on my head and said, "Well now, snowflake," or maybe, "Hello there, snowflake."

I didn't know what he was talking about, so I just smiled up at him. But Mama was angry in a flash. "His name is not Snowflake," she said through tight lips. "His name is Ben—and please keep your hands off his head." And she flounced off in a huff, dragging me along. I had no idea at that time why she became so angry.

Another instance that sticks in my memory, but again without emotion as far as I can recall, occurred in Little League baseball. I was twelve or thirteen, I believe, and made an all-star, interracial team as pitcher. When we went up to the town of Leakey to compete with another all-star team, I spent most of the time warming up back behind the stands and out of sight. I never did get to play. But I didn't get upset. In fact, I paid little attention to the matter even when someone later explained, "The people in Leakey don't like black folks very much." At least it explained why I had spent so much time out back "warming up."

However, in my home town of Uvalde, we kids didn't experience enough of that to bother about, or at least we weren't aware of it if it happened.

* * *

Two episodes stand out when I press my mind back into the wells of deepest memory, one embarrassing and bewildering, the other eerie and Faulkneresque.

The first episode was very short. I was standing out in the yard when Mama came charging out the door, yelling just once. She ripped a switch off a nearby pecan tree and gave me a hard thrashing. I remember it vividly to this day. Right out there in broad daylight in front of the neighborhood she gave me a good switching. I mean, she wore me out!

The odd thing is that, as vividly as I remember the incident—and I must have been nine or ten years old—I don't recall the reason. I'm sure I knew at the time, and it must have been significant because Mama always had good reasons for what she did. But I sure remember the whipping.

The second incident runs on in my mind much differently. It's almost in slow motion, a bit confusing, somewhat otherworldly, like one of the avant-garde Italian films of the sixties. I was about three years old, too young to be in school, and I was staying with my aunt during the day while my mother taught school at Nicolas Street just a block away. I was sitting in the dust of Nicolas Street, a little-used road, and I was playing with a little bucket and digging in the dirt, amusing myself contentedly.

Gradually I became aware of a commotion some distance away. Someone was yelling. I played in the dirt. The yelling increased, and motion crept into my consciousness. I looked up and saw Barney running down the road toward me. Barney was a young black man, nineteen or twenty years old, one of the people who lived in the neighborhood. He was running toward me, yelling and waving his arms. And people were running behind him. They were screaming, too. There were men and women. And they were chasing Barney. He was coming straight toward me. I was aware that he was barefooted and shirtless.

This all happened very quickly, but it seemed stretched

out and lazy, like a slow motion film. I played in the dirt. I gazed at the wild, waving runners for a few seconds. Then I played in the dirt some more. Once when I looked up, I thought I saw Mama running up the street behind Barney. I played some more.

In a few moments Barney reached me, and he abruptly stopped and bent over and began to play in the dirt with me. He stopped yelling and the expression on his face became very peaceful. Only his heavy breathing broke the immediate stillness.

But then I heard Mama's screaming voice, and I looked up. Yes, she was one of those running toward us. She was waving and yelling, just like the others. I waved, too. Barney looked up, and the expression on his face changed again. He bolted to his feet and began running down the street away from the approaching gang. There were only three or four frantic people, but it seemed like a gang to me. Barney ran as hard as he could and began yelling again.

That was the day Barney went crazy. He simply came apart and never did recover. I guess everybody had been afraid he was going to harm me, but he was as gentle as anyone could be. He just played in the dirt with me.

* * *

Christmas was always a special time in our home. Mama, of course, was openly committed to Jesus Christ, a believer in every sense of the word and a steady churchgoer. Daddy was not a believer at the time and preferred baseball to churchgoing. But he was a traditionalist in many ways, a man of sentiment and respect for others. He was not without fault, but he was definitely a family man.

The happiest moment I can remember from those early years of childhood in Uvalde came at Christmas time. It seems insignificant in hindsight, but it was important at the time. It was the day before Christmas, and Daddy brought home some new lights for our Christmas tree. They were big, round, fluorescent bulbs. I had never seen lights like that. They glowed and turned that little tree into the grandest thing I'd ever seen. I was flooded with delight and expectation.

I remember almost nothing else about that particular Christmas. I don't even remember the presents. But I remember staring at those bulbs that Daddy had brought, and I can remember going to bed and lying there with my eyes wide open for what seemed like hours. I was actually afraid to go to sleep for fear I might die before Christmas morning came. "Now you just watch," I said to myself. "You just watch me die tonight. All those good things are going to happen tomorrow on Christmas and I'll die and miss everything."

I didn't, of course, and it turned out to be a very good Christmas. But the struggle between feelings of security and a developing inferiority complex were well underway. The seeds of stress and turmoil had been planted by some alien hand. As they grew, they struggled constantly to crowd out the warmth and love so often demonstrated by my mom and dad. Looking back, I have no doubt whatsoever that they loved me, and I can only remember one argument between the two of them. Yet, being a human in a fallen world, I had a hard time holding onto the feeling of being loved.

3

What's Wrong with Me?

BIG PAPA HAD BEEN LIVING WITH US for some time. He was my mother's father. He moved into the middle bedroom and when he was sick, there was never a question that Mama would take care of him, and I never heard Daddy complain about it. Big Papa simply became part of the family.

He was a fairly heavy drinker, and I remember that this was painful for Mama. At times he would go off for days and hire out as a cook for sheepshearers or deerhunters. I remember the first time I noticed what would become a peculiar pattern developing.

Son, McGee, Kitsy, and I were playing out in our make-believe world on the rear side yard. Suddenly we heard Big Papa's loud voice, announcing his homecoming from a cooking stint for some sheepshearers. He usually talked loud and had a hard, raucous laugh. The three of us looked up, and he spotted us.

"Hey, you kids!" he yelled. "Hey, come on over here and see what I have for you."

We jumped up and eagerly ran over to the backyard near the screened porch and Big Papa laughed loudly again, lightly pummeling Son and McGee and mussing Kitsy's hair. He was always rubbing their heads with his big, rough hands, but he seldom touched me. I was aware at that moment that he touched the others, but he didn't touch me. He glanced at me every now and then, I thought, and he sometimes seemed to stare into my eyes. But he hardly ever showed physical affection to me as he did the others.

"Hey, look here!" he said, and thrust his hard hand into his right pants pocket. It was bulging. He came out with several shiny coins. They were silver dollars. I couldn't believe it. I'd never seen so many. He tossed them in his hand and laughed, teasingly, and began to hand them out to Son, McGee, and Kitsy. He gave them two apiece, and they giggled and jumped up and down. Then he looked at me. "Here you go, Ben!" He handed me one silver dollar.

I thought, *I wonder why he gave them two, and me only one?* But a silver dollar was a silver dollar.

As the weeks and months passed and the scene was repeated with only slight variations, the question deepened. *Doesn't he like me as much as them? What's wrong with me? Why doesn't he ever touch me? He just looks at me.*

My three cousins always got at least two silver dollars every time he went sheepshearing. I never remember getting more than one, and there were occasions when Big Papa was drinking that he passed me over altogether. I never was able to figure it out. I knew only that Big Papa, my grandfather, appeared not to like me. I later learned that he seemed to show partiality among his own children, preferring my mother's brothers to her. But to my child's mind, I felt he didn't like me and I didn't know why.

As the years passed, Big Papa would say, more than once—perhaps in jest, perhaps in earnest—"That boy, Ben, will end up in jail before he's twenty years old." I never understood why he would say that, either.

Even before these episodes with my grandfather I'd had flashes of uneasiness about myself. Why was I always being passed around from aunt to aunt? In my earliest memories, that seemed to be the case. The answer was fairly simple actually. My mother was teaching school, or she was off to summer school to further her education, or she was helping someone in need. And I spent the summers first with this aunt and then with another.

In Uvalde when Mama worked, I stayed a lot with my old-maid Aunt Minnie. Though she suffered from severe arthritis, she was kind and loving. But she was not my mother.

I spent a lot of time with my aunt up in Pearsall, a little farming town noted for its watermelons, cantaloupes, and peanuts. She had four children—Sonny, Regge, Ann, and Myrtle Jo—and we got along fine, but it wasn't home.

Where did I belong? Now, this was not a constant question. I didn't sit around and think about it. But it crept into my mind in quiet moments, maybe before I dropped off to sleep or after an especially difficult day, or maybe early in the morning as I was getting dressed and thought about home.

Actually, I *did* understand. My mother wasn't neglecting me; in my conscious mind I knew that. She worked harder than anyone I knew. So did Daddy. They were constantly striving to make our life better. But still, I was a drifter—here a few days, over there the next, at home awhile. No one else, it seemed to me, had to do that. Why did I? Why couldn't I be at home like Son, Kitsy, McGee, and all my other cousins? It seemed to me that everyone got to stay home but me.

Part of my confusion lay in the fact that I was more than likely an overly sensitive kid. Society is often quick to use that word, sensitive, and it has become rather meaningless, or it is understood to mean sissy or effeminate. But in my case, I believe, I responded more quickly and more deeply to outside stimuli than most children of my age and circumstance. A word, an action, a look that rolled right off most others would land on me like a ton of bricks. I took, or mistook, too many acts as criticism of me.

When people don't feel good about themselves, almost anything can be taken as an insult. Children especially have no frame of reference or sense of perspective. Parents need to be careful what they say or do around children. We need to tell them often that they have value and worth and are loved. I do not remember as a child anyone ever saying things like, "Ben, you're great! I love you."

And in my estimation of myself, I felt there was plenty to be critical about. For one thing, I was a tall kid—skinny, frail, gawky, funny-looking, with a head that was too little and feet that were too big. Although I was still too young to be deeply concerned, I felt that girls never liked me—at least, not the pretty ones. A lot of my friends seemed so much more graceful, sophisticated, and witty.

When I started to grow, I was quickly taller than other kids, and this compounded matters. I remember that my baseball caps always seemed to be too big and my mother would have to notch them in back. They always looked funny. And my pants were too short. My baseball uniform looked silly— the pants often barely covered my knees while everybody else's came down long and looked so graceful. My socks failed to reach my knees, while those of my team mates came up nice and high and fit smoothly under their trouser legs.

I can remember the day I graduated from the eighth grade. It may have been my first full-blown concern about appearance and style apart from the sports field. That graduation was a big event for our school. The superintendent of all the schools, a white man of course, came to speak and exhort us to go out and make something of ourselves.

But the one thing that stands out in my memory of that event was that Johnny Boy, a kid in my class, got a new suit for the occasion. I didn't have a new suit. He did. Why? Sure, it was from J. C. Penney's, but it was a new suit. He looked smooth. I felt tall, rumpled, skinny, and awkward.

Later, I became one of those "pretty boys." I had a pretty face, round, smooth, wide-eyed. And that caused real problems. I was too skinny and frail to fight anyone who called me "Pretty Boy" or "Sissy" or anything like that. Furthermore, Mama would land all over me if I got into a fight. So I fell back upon the resources of the mind. I tried to outsmart everyone: I became clever, a talker, a salesman type. Deception was not far down the road.

* * *

Psychoanalyzing oneself is usually a fruitless pastime, primarily because it calls for total honesty, which few have a capacity for. But, all in all, I don't believe I was a maladjusted child. Fundamentally I was a happy boy and got along well with all the kids. I wanted to be like them. And that was the problem. Somehow I felt I couldn't be like them. I felt different, maybe even an oddball in some respects. But in those early days, this sense—this "knowledge"—came only in momentary flashes.

The scary part is that those traces of insecurity were there—in my inner being, in my heart as the Bible says, and they were gradually forcing their way to the surface. "As [a man] thinketh in his heart," said Solomon, "so is he."[1] What is in the inner being will come out; it will dominate. The person will eventually live out those things that come from the heart, whether it be greed or lust or insecurity.

It isn't what you say or do on the outside that is real, because we can control outward appearances. We want people to think well of us so we hide the "real me." This is why God "looks on the inner man" . . . where it is impossible to hide.

How do traces of insecurity take root in us? We know those feelings are not planted by the One who made us. They originate elsewhere. They really are like little seeds, little beginnings—a thought, an idea, an impression, a fear, a momentary acceptance of the possibility.

Parents, watch what you say to your children. Praise them. Love them. Congratulate them when they do well. Don't continually harp on their mistakes. Give long praises, short criticisms, and follow a spanking with a hug. Don't leave the child to go off to quiet his tears without the knowledge that he is loved.

We find no evidence in the account of creation that man experienced any insecurity or fear in his initial relationship with God, his Creator. Quite the contrary, the relationship was completely open and harmonious. As the specific creation of God, man had authority over the rest of creation. He and God knew one another intimately. We glimpse the harmony and security of that time in these words from the Scriptures: "And they heard the voice of the Lord God walking in the garden in the cool of the day. . . . And the Lord God called unto Adam . . . Where art thou?"[2]

Here we read of God Himself—the Sovereign of creation—coming down to walk, talk, visit man: "And God blessed them, and God said unto them, Be fruitful, and multiply, and replenish the earth, and subdue it: and have dominion over the fish of the sea, and over the fowl of the air, and over every living thing that moveth upon the earth. . . . And God saw every thing that he had made, and, behold it was very good."[3]

We further sense the love and compassion in the relationship in God's concern for man's total well-being. "It is not good," He said, "that the man should be alone; I will make him an help meet for him."[4] In the more detailed account of the creation of woman, there is no hint of fear, no warped sensitivity or inadequacy in the words that were left for us so that we might understand God's love and ourselves:

> And the Lord God caused a deep sleep to fall upon Adam, and he slept: and he took one of his ribs, and closed up the flesh instead thereof;
> And the rib, which the Lord God had taken from man, made he a woman, and brought her unto the man.
> And Adam said, This is now bone of my bones, and flesh of my flesh: she shall be called Woman, because she was taken out of Man.
> Therefore shall a man leave his father and his mother, and shall cleave unto his wife: and they shall be one flesh.
> And they were both naked, the man and his wife, and *were not ashamed.*[5]

They were innocent, harmless, and blameless. They were without fear or shame. They stood tall before God and the rest of creation—until the day came when they thumbed their nose at the arrangement. Then we see the traces of insecurity and fear creep in. "And Adam and his wife hid themselves from the presence of the Lord God amongst the trees of the garden."[6] The conflict of the ages was set in motion. Man is still hiding himself among the trees from the presence of the Lord God.

Man once so strong—with dominion and authority—became weak and helpless when he decided he would disobey God. He actually kicked the support out from under himself, and fell. We all know how it happened. The serpent, the devil, deceived the woman, and then the man through the woman, into violating God's instructions regarding the fruit of the tree of the knowledge of good and evil that stood in the midst of the Garden of Eden. Beguiled by the lies of the serpent, Eve tasted the fruit and enticed Adam to try it: "And the eyes of them both were opened, and they knew that they were naked; and they sewed fig leaves together, and made themselves aprons."[7]

Having once been unashamed about their nakedness and secure in their condition, they suddenly wanted to hide it. They could not stand to be exposed before God, recognizing that their nakedness that once revealed purity suddenly represented their sin. So what did they do? They took man's first "religious" step, trying to cover up sin with their own works, making garments for themselves.

Fear had entered the universe—and the heart and life of man. It was not from God. It was from the one described in the Scriptures as the father of lies[8] and the accuser of the brethren—God's adversary, Satan.[9]

As a result, man had to leave the Garden of Eden, the place of perfect security and peace. God "drove out the man," the Bible says.[10] Sorrow took hold, paradise was lost, and man was to travail and struggle in life.[11] Where once the creation brought forth only good, now it was to produce thorns and thistles.[12] Life would be hard, man would endure sickness and disease, he would suffer physically, mentally, and spiritually. And, little boys would be vulnerable to insecurity as the twentieth-century world unfolded.

* * *

The last thing I want to do is to appear to blame someone else for allowing the seeds of insecurity and fear to take root in me. Especially would I not want to blame my mother who struggled with so much in those days. But I remember well an oft-repeated incident that probably fed those roots and contributed to the growth of the ridiculously frightened inner man, the one no one knew about but me. It is an incident that might even seem funny when viewed from an adult perspective.

It was nighttime. Mama and I were at home alone. I was probably seven or eight years old, full of energy, restless, running back and forth, yammering endlessly. Mama was absolutely worn out, as she was so often, from her relentless schedule of working hard at home, teaching school, and studying long hours to improve herself. How she handled it all, I'll never know. But here I was, wound up and exploding with energy while she needed peace and quiet. As I was racing around the room like a six-week-old puppy, she suddenly stopped and said, "Shh! Do you hear that?" She was perfectly still, wide-eyed and intent. She said it again, "Shh! What's that?"

I went absolutely rigid, and I thought my eyes might pop out of my head. I looked at her. "What is it?"

She cocked her head to one side. "Can you hear it?" she asked me.

I didn't say anything, but I was sure I had heard it. "What is it?" I asked again.

She lowered her voice to a hissing whisper. "It's the loup-garou."

"The what?" I could barely hear my own voice.

"The loup-garou."

"What's that?"

"It's out there in the dark. Hear him dragging his tail through the weeds? We'd better be quiet so he doesn't know we're in here."

And that was that. You wouldn't hear a peep out of me for the rest of the night. I might not sleep much, but I remained quiet, listening for that loup-garou's tail dragging in the weeds out there in the dark. It worked that first night, and quite understandably my mother fell back on the device many times during my super active youth.

I didn't know that *loup-garou* was French for "werewolf." I didn't have to. To me it was a nameless terror that knew all about me. I couldn't see it, but it could see me. And there was nothing I could do about it.

I'm afraid parents do that to their children all the time. Inadvertently, they establish weakness in their children, whom they genuinely love.

In my case, I grew up with a subconscious fear of the dark that haunted me for many years, traceable perhaps to the incident of the loup-garou. It showed up also as a fear of making myself a target for whatever I couldn't touch and see. It was a deep insecurity ultimately, founded on silliness, but nonetheless real and powerful enough to warp a fallen human personality.

As I headed toward major change in my life, those early traces of doubts about myself—which more and more posed the question of "What's wrong with me?"—would be a critical factor.

4

The City

ALL DURING MY YEARS AT NICOLAS Street School, I looked forward to the day when I would play football for the Uvalde High School Coyotes. My dad was their biggest fan; he seldom missed a game. And my greatest expectation was to play ball and make my dad proud. My dreams, the nighttime ones and the wide-awake ones, were filled with fabulous gridiron exploits, with myself right in the middle of each game-deciding play.

So it was a rude awakening when I learned that, because I was black, I would not be able to attend Uvalde High School. And if you didn't attend Uvalde High School, you didn't play for the Coyotes. With hindsight, I'm sure there had been conversation about segregation as I was growing up, but in my naïveté I must have closed my ears to it. I fully expected to go to high school there. I was a natural-born Coyote.

That was my first definitive encounter with segregation. And the realization of difference broke upon me. Because I was "colored," I was different.

Sure, when we had gone to the movies as little kids, we sat in the balcony. But none of us wanted to sit downstairs anyway. Upstairs you could look down on everyone and throw popcorn, bags, and boxes down on the people below. The Mexicans all sat up there, and even some of the white kids liked to be where the fun was. We'd buy our "balcony" tickets and the usher would say, "Upstairs," and we went right up the stairs without thinking about it.

Uvalde didn't have a large black population and apparently was unusual in its day-to-day relationships between races. Youngsters didn't pay a lot of attention to skin color anyway. We were all different. The whites were pale and washed out, the Mexicans were a little darker, and we were darker than any of them. Even we blacks were all different shades of brown and black.

So people called us colored. It meant nothing.

I remember we used to tease the little white and Mexican kids. We would get in shouting matches with them, throwing rocks harmlessly. "You know what?" we'd yell. "You're a nigger and I'm not!" We didn't have the foggiest idea what we were yelling. I didn't know what it meant. I guess our parents had shielded us from most of the ugliness of racism.

So now there was a racial problem in Uvalde. What were they going to do with the eight of us in my class? There was no black high school, and we would not be allowed to attend the white school. The problem had never been dealt with on a group basis before. Black families with kids going into high school had taken care of the matter individually. A handful, those with great determination like my mother, had found ways to go to school elsewhere; most others dropped out. But this time, the black parents were pressing to have the school board deal with all eight of us together, as a class.

First they said they would transport us daily to Bracketville, which had the closest black high school, but it was forty-four miles each way. Our parents said no. Eighty-eight miles a day in an old school bus was too much. Talk about busing. . . .

Finally all parties agreed—our parents reluctantly—on a plan to place the eight of us in a boarding school in San Antonio, eighty-six miles east of Uvalde. It was a private school for blacks operated by the Roman Catholic Church.

* * *

So this is St. Peter Claver's Academy, I thought upon my arrival there that fall in 1951. For the teenager, there are "the rules of being cool." Rule One was, Never allow yourself to be impressed. So I kept my expression appropriately bored and pronounced, "Some dump."

It wasn't exactly a dump, just very institutional. Two big nondescript brick buildings and two separated yards, one for boys, one for girls. The girls lived in a walled-off side of the first building while the nuns lived in the other half. The boys lived in the second building, a big house across the street from the first. Two nuns lived downstairs.

This was my first serious time away from home except for the visits with various aunts during the summers and I was impressed in spite of Rule One. This was big time! *It will be okay,* I thought.

And that first Friday, Saturday, and Sunday were okay. We hung around and had a good time. The school was on the east side of San Antonio, a community of about a quarter of a million people in those days. It was in an interracial section of that then-segregated city.

The Uvalde Eight were wide-eyed over the big town, for it seemed massive to country bumpkins like us. And we were country—totally unsophisticated, transparent, and fresh. I, for example, had been told by my parents, particularly my mother, that I was going to San Antonio to study. "You get into those books," Mama instructed with tight-lipped serious-ness. "Don't you mess around and waste time. You study and learn."

Now there were two things you didn't do at my house, and both of them were, Don't argue with Mama. It simply was not done. In fact, this was the case in most of the "good" black families I was acquainted with around Uvalde. You did not hear youngsters talking back to their parents. It never occurred to me to try it. The first obstacle to that was Mama herself. She was demanding, and she was tough. But the sec-ond obstacle was Daddy. His presence hovered over every-thing. I figured the worst thing that could happen to me was to have Mama *not* whip me but turn me over to Daddy in-stead. Actually, that never happened. His powerful presence was enough. I didn't know what he might do if he ever had to administer corporal punishment, but I was convinced it would be horrible. My young mind went numb at the thought.

That was an important ingredient in black family life. In all the homes that I look back on, I find only one or two cases where the man was not in charge. He may not have been very smart or well educated, but he was in charge. His presence dominated life in the household. And in all those homes, there was stability. There were problems, there was poverty, and there was pain, but there was a certain evenness and order to life.

So when my parents said, "We want you to do your lessons," there was no court of higher appeal. I was not to fool around. I did my lessons.

Those first exploratory days at St. Peter Claver's Academy were fascinating and innocent.

* * *

It was Monday morning, 6 A.M. Somebody was shaking my arm. I snapped awake—and I didn't know where I was. Someone was looking into my face. It wasn't Mama. It was someone white, a white woman, I thought, but I wasn't sure. She had this strange thing on her head. In a second I got my bearings, and I knew it was one of the nuns.

"Get up, fellow," she said softly but evenly. "We must go and make a mess." She had a strong Irish accent.

"Huh?"

She said it again. "Get up, fellow, we must go and make a mess."

I blinked my eyes and tried to focus. "A mess? Well, I guess if they want a mess, I'll get up and go make a mess with them." I didn't know what else to do. I climbed out of bed, still a bit wobbly and uncertain. In the washroom, I asked one of the other guys, "Hey, what's this mess we're gonna make?"

He looked at me as though I were an idiot and the fellow at the next washbasin broke up in gales of laughter. "It's not a mess, dummy, it's a *mass.*"

"Oh," I looked into the mirror. "A mass, huh?"

"Yeah, dummy, a mass—like church."

* * *

Mass—fifty or sixty sleepy black kids of all ages up through high school and a dozen or so white nuns along with a white priest robed in colorful vestments. My only experience with the Roman Catholic mass had been back home at the Mexican church where our gang would go on New Year's Eve as an excuse to stay out late. But in San Antonio that Monday morning, it was different. We were suddenly up close, right in the middle, expected to participate. My eyes were bugging.

It was quite dark. The boys were on one side and the girls on the other. The seats were hard. And this guy came out of a little room on the side, with two little guys behind him— all in "dresses." And this first guy, the priest, stood there in front of the altar with his back to us and started speaking in some strange language, every now and then moving his hands and bobbing his head and kneeling. And then one of the kids rang a bell and everybody stood up. I jumped up quickly, not wanting to miss anything. Then suddenly everybody dropped to his knees again. The priest turned around to face us and said, "O Remos," and everybody else said something like, "Et come spirit to-two." That sort of thing went on and on. I was lost. "What is this?" I stuttered under my breath. I was terrified, fascinated, awed. "What are they *doing?*" I wondered. I was going to have to get the hang of all this.

Sometimes they would celebrate high mass, and the girls would sit up in the balcony and they and the priest would sing most of the service. I thought that was remarkable, too. I'd never seen anything like it.

Two weeks passed, and I had seen just about everything they were going to do during mass. The priest seemed to do the same thing every morning Monday through Friday and then again on Sunday. We also attended novenas on Wednesday nights and then confession on Fridays. I liked confession. I figured I could do pretty much as I pleased all week and then go in on Friday and get cleaned up for another week. The priest would impose a few penances, I'd say a few "Hail, Marys"—I got really fast at saying them—and then off I'd go.

As I settled into the routine, it got boring and I began to have a hard time staying awake for early morning mass. I decided to watch the nuns. I figured I might learn from them what was so wonderful about mass so I wouldn't have so much trouble staying awake.

One morning, I sat toward the back, close to one of the sisters. Her habit had long, full sleeves and I noticed she tucked her hands up inside the sleeves in a reverent manner. She knelt in a peculiar way, with her elbows on the back of the next pew. That allowed her to sit, more than kneel. She was just sort of kneeling forward with her haunches still on the seat. That was a lot more comfortable, it seemed to me, than trying to stay erect and put all your weight on your knees. "Maybe that's the way you worship," I said to myself, so I tried it. I didn't have the long sleeves, but I folded my hands around my forearms and clasped them together. Then I checked the sister again.

She had her head down with her forehead resting on the back of the pew in front of her. And she was very still. *That must be the way to do it,* I thought, and I slid forward with my haunches on the edge of the seat and rested my forehead on the pew in front of me.

I soon realized her very worshipful posture was conducive to dozing, and one morning shortly after that I heard sister snoring softly. She wasn't praying, she was sleeping! I had fought like crazy against dropping off to sleep in those early, dark mornings. I had assumed God was watching, and He'd see me there sleeping, and hit me with one of those bolts of lightning people talked about. But then I said, "If she can sleep through mass . . . I can, too." From then on, I slept through most of the masses I attended the rest of my four years at St. Peter Claver's Academy.

From mass each morning, we marched right into breakfast in the dining hall where they served us milk and day-old sweet rolls. I learned that a local bakery gave the school a good price on day-old products and so, every morning we had sweet rolls. They weren't bad, though.

From breakfast, we marched into catechism class. Every youngster had his day to say the rosary, and I remember really sweating to try to master the five mysteries and all the other points of doctrine we were supposed to memorize. Day-old sweet rolls and learning rosaries do not go together well.

One fact stuck with me through all this—the Catholics were serious about their religion. No Methodist or Baptist I knew went to church every day, much less memorized all the liturgy and key points of faith. No one lit all those candles and said all those confessions, week in and week out. These people meant business.

* * *

It didn't take us long to discover that we were only six blocks from "Gunga Din"—the strip where the black pimps, prostitutes, hustlers, and gangsters of that section of town hung out. Every kind of bar, nightclub, and joint imaginable could be found, all segregated except for a few whites looking for some action.

Before long we were heading there frequently, after school for a couple of hours and on the weekends. At first we country boys just stood and watched. It seemed glamorous to us. This was real life. Uvalde faded more and more into the past.

The first thing I learned was the necessity to be "cool." If Rule One was, Never be impressed, Rule Two was, Be cool. There had been nothing cool about those of us from Uvalde. We had to learn how to be "laid back," relaxed to the point of drowsiness. The point was to secure the high ground and look down on everyone else, aloof, arrogant, untouchable. We learned quickly from the junkies and hustlers on the street that everyone had an angle. "Everybody is out to get you, so you've got to be cool. Eat or be eaten; get or get got— survival is the name of the game."

It made sense to me, so I began to practice being cool. I saw that there was a certain way to stand, for instance. You always put one hand in your pants pocket and raised the other up to the lapel area if you were wearing a jacket and you sort of gripped the lapel. Or if you weren't wearing a jacket, you just held your hand up close to your chin. And you had to hold a handkerchief in the raised hand, a few inches from your mouth. You sort of talked into the handkerchief, frequently daubing your mouth with it. And you never spoke loudly. You whispered softly, hoarsely, "Hey, man, what's happening?" daubing at your mouth with your handkerchief. That was cool.

Soon I was as cool as anyone on the street.

It wasn't long until I learned what was "happening." Those

people spoke into handkerchiefs and wiped at their mouths because they were drooling or their noses were running as a result of the heroin they were using. The handkerchiefs, which looked so cool, were a cover-up. The laid-back talk and the low voice also stemmed from drug use. They were literally on the verge of falling asleep—"nodding out." They were loaded—"high"—too far gone to speak any louder.

I fell for the cool routine, but by the mercy of God I didn't fall heavily into drug use. I know that my mother's insistence on studying, which I took seriously at least in the beginning, helped. I loved sports, too, and that also helped. For as we picked up our street smarts, we immediately learned about marijuana. Everybody "did joints"—smoked grass, pot, weed, tea. It was as common as ordinary cigarettes or Coca Cola®. I tried it, but it did not become a habit for me.

Even so, I learned the words, the gross language, the thought processes, the lust, the self-concern. I learned the conceit. I learned the con-man's style. I learned manipulation.

And I also learned the hard way about alcohol. In Uvalde, I had never drunk anything stronger than Coke. I remember drinking one beer and getting high as Cooty Brown.

One of the first things we did after arriving at St. Peter Claver's Academy and hitting the streets was to steal a case of beer. A guy we met there actually stole it from a parked beer truck. The driver was on the other side of the vehicle, preparing to unload some of his product, and this fellow darted over, grabbed the case, swung it onto his back and started running. The driver came around the truck in time to see him, yelled, and started chasing him. But that kid, with the beer on his back and all of us running in front of him, outran the driver and made it back to the school. We ran around to the side of the dormitory, up the fire escape, and through a window. We consumed the beer in short order, laughing, giggling, yelling, and congratulating ourselves, but we didn't get caught.

And then there was "WPLJ," a curse for many, many black people, young and old. We learned about that, too—white port and lemon juice. You obtained the cheapest wine possible, port or muscatel, a couple of gallons if you had a good-sized group in your party. Then you bought some little cans of lemon juice. First you "killed the poison," following an old superstition of pouring off the top. Then you drank some of the wine until you emptied it to the point where you could add a can or two of lemon juice. You shook it and drank. When it got low, you added more juice.

We did this on the streets, standing there, being cool, daubing our mouths, and getting drunk. But it didn't stop there.

I remember the time when a gang of us returned to the dormitory after a session like this. We all were in bad shape, a dozen or more of us, and we threw bottles, cans, and all sorts of garbage out the window into the yard and even down the stairs to the nuns' living quarters. And some of us became drastically sick, vomiting all over the place. Enough WPLJ could turn a sane, sound young man into the sickest, weakest, most disgusting person imaginable.

Late that Saturday afternoon, I had my first encounter with an angry nun. She, with another sister, was in charge of the boys' dormitory. Sister came up the stairs, saw us and stopped dead still at the top of the landing, her face frozen. Then her face became red and the veins stood out. Her normally thin mouth was like a slash. Her teeth, which were small to begin with, didn't show at all. And she fell into a rage.

"You little beasts!" she hissed. "You're just little animals! *Animals!*" She lost control, understandably. She had not appeared to like us very much anyway. She was tough and stern. But that day, I would guess, she hated us, at least momentarily.

* * *

I was on a youthful roller coaster by that time. I still had traces of my upbringing and warnings about studying echoing in my ears, but I was sliding fast and I was learning about the real world in a hurry.

Probably my biggest surprise was discovering homosexuality. In addition to the nuns, we had one clergyman for a teacher. He taught eighth grade and was in charge of the boys' dormitory. He slept there. And he was a homosexual.

I didn't have any idea what a homosexual was; I had never encountered one in Uvalde. We joked about sissies and stuff but here was a man of authority in a building full of young boys and it didn't take long to discover his ways. Actually he and two upper class students always hung around together. This teacher who was "kind and good" took me to hear my first symphony and to a number of parties.

I recall one day during a performance of one of the many operettas we staged at St. Peter Claver's. Our principal was crazy about Gilbert and Sullivan operettas, and we were forever doing one. In this particular case, we were doing "The Pirates of Penzance." I was in the make-up room getting ready to play the Prince of the Pirates, and the director, a layman, was helping us get ready. My turn came, and he began applying my make-up. Then I was aware that he was close to my face, and he stroked it slowly, smiling sweetly. "It's going to be hard to make you ugly."

I can remember muttering, "Well, well—him, too!"

I gradually learned that a number of the youngsters there had fallen into this. You could spot them, the teacher and the kids, and if you were smart, you could play them along for money, for the use of their cars, and things like that. You could get away without paying up for a long time, but eventually there was a price to pay for the favors.

It was a subtle thing, but this kind of experience—the sporadic falling away from parental discipline, the homosexual encounters, the inability to attract a "real" girlfriend—steadily chipped away at my already exposed flaw, insecurity. I increasingly asked myself, "What is wrong with me?" I was sort of half here and half there. I didn't seem to belong anywhere wholeheartedly. The question gnawed at me for two years at the San Antonio school.

* * *

A significant break came at the end of my sophomore year. Despite my shenanigans, I had persisted significantly in my quest for good grades. I might mess up now and then, but I couldn't forget my mother's stern warnings for long. So I studied.

I vividly remember receiving my report card. All the grades were A's. But that wasn't all. That was the year they gave us I.Q. tests. And they called out the scores in class. It was unbelievable. Everyone knew what everyone else scored. And I was second from the top.

When class let out, we all went down into the school yard.

The girls' yard, paved and surrounded by a high fence to keep the boys out, was at the rear of the school building. The boys' yard, unpaved but also surrounded by a high fence, was across the street in front of the building.

As I came down the front steps, I glanced across the street into the boys' yard and there, under a big tree near the entrance where they always stood, were "Prez" and his gang. They were the cool dudes, the hipsters, the ones who ran things on campus and hung out together on the streets. They were usually snorting or skin-popping heroin, standing around drowsily, looking cool, daubing their mouths with handkerchiefs, talking hoarsely just above a whisper. Periodically the identity of "Prez" changed as the school authorities cracked down and expelled the worst offenders, but a new Prez always emerged.

As I came down the stairs and headed for the yard, I heard a loud voice. "Hey, Baby, here come the brain!" Raucous laughter, then other voices joined in. "Here come the brain! Here come the brain! Yeah, Man, he the brain. Hey, Brain, what's happenin'? What's two plus two, Brain? Haw-haw!"

From anyone else, the remarks might have been construed to be complimentary. From the Prez and his cohorts, they were a definite put-down. They were ridiculing me for having excelled. The one thing you don't do is excel in "straight action" in front of people like the Prez and his gang.

Feeling completely isolated at that moment, I made a once-for-all decision that this would be the last time anyone laughed at me. The crack of insecurity within me burst wide open. I was not going to be ridiculed again. I was not going to be "weird" any longer. I was going to be one of the guys.

From that point on, my grades did a nosedive. I stopped applying myself altogether. By the end of my four years at the academy, I was fortunate not to have been suspended. The authorities at the school telephoned my parents. But nothing made any difference to me. I had decided.

* * *

Psychologists and sociologists have for a long time recognized the hazards of peer pressure. They continually warn parents and society of those dangers. I personally feel the

dangers are underestimated. Pressure to conform in our day—
and presumably in every day throughout history—is one of
the great curses of man. It produces warped character of every
kind and degree imaginable. Envy, jealousy, greed, anger,
hatred, and crime can all be traced back to seeds deriving
from pressure to conform to the world or the age in which
we live.

Yet the psychologists and sociologists do not seem to offer
many solutions to this internal problem of man. They merely
identify it. I would be well along in mid-life before I would
discover someone who offered a solution. It was found in the
Bible.

Paul, the apostle, gave the key in a letter he wrote to the
Christians at Rome. Romans is the amazing epistle that revolu-
tionized the Christian church after Martin Luther probed it
to the very essence of all things. There he discovered the
truth that man is justified before God by faith in Jesus Christ,
who was sent to pay the penalty for sin by dying on a cross.
Good works did not save a man; faith in Christ did. In that
letter, Paul wrote two sentences that drive to the heart of
man's uncontrollable need to conform: "I beseech you therefore, brethren, by the mercies of God, that ye present your
bodies a living sacrifice, holy, acceptable unto God, which is
your reasonable service. And *be not conformed to this world:
but be ye transformed by the renewing of your mind,* that
ye may prove what is that good, and acceptable, and perfect,
will of God."[1]

The apostle was showing how to break the bondage to the
curse of the age. "Give yourselves unreservedly to Almighty
God," he said in effect. "Hold nothing back—no part of yourself, your family, your job, your past, your present, your future.
Give it to the Lord, not as *dead* sacrifice, when you die, but
as a present, living, lively sacrifice."

Once that has been done, Paul said, the bond is broken.
You are free from the human drive to conform. The chain
is smashed, and you are free to conform to God, the only
free Being in the universe. You, too, become free. The Holy
Spirit can then lead you in every aspect of life, giving you
full expression of everything that God intended you to be.

No longer will you find it necessary to conform to the Joneses, the Rockefellers, or even to the Prez and his gang.

Jesus Himself said it in much the same way to the people who were beginning to believe in Him as the Son of God and Savior of the world: "Then said Jesus to those Jews which believed on him, If ye continue in my word, then are ye my disciples indeed; And ye shall know the truth, and the truth shall make you free."[2]

He was speaking of the entire bondage of sin, which ultimately weighs down upon every aspect of life and directs the course of mankind. He reinforced the solution a few sentences later when He declared: "If the Son therefore shall make you free, ye shall be free indeed."[3]

Fortunately, even at the lowest point of my deterioration as a student at St. Peter Claver's Academy, I never went all the way to the center of the Prez's circle. I dabbled on the fringes, but managed, by the sheer grace of God, to avoid drug use and stay out of jail. Despite my determination never to be ridiculed again for being smart or different, I still remained somewhat set apart. I couldn't be like Prez all the way, even when I was with the gang. I was always different. The cloud of insecurity lightened from time to time, but it never vanished. I found out later there were a lot of us; some just fought it harder than others. They became the inner circle.

I found a way to let off steam through athletics, to which I earnestly devoted myself. As had been shown in Uvalde's Little League, I was a pretty good baseball pitcher, good enough that a scout for the old St. Louis Browns expressed interest in helping me go to the University of Illinois when I graduated from high school and to enter the Browns' farm system. I never followed through on that, but athletics remained central to my young life.

There was basketball, which would return to prominence in my later experiences, and there was football, which was important in high school. Oddly, I played center in the old single-wing football system we used at that time. I was tall by then, still gangly, but steadily putting on weight.

I well remember a game in Corpus Christi, Texas. I was alternating at center with another guy. During a break in the action, we were standing on the sidelines, and I noticed he was crying.

"Hey, Man, what's the matter?" I asked.

"That guy keeps hitting me," he said.

"What guy?"

"That big s.o.b. in front of me. He keeps punching me. Everytime I snap the ball, he hits me right in the face," he blurted.

"Well, hit him back," I said, hoping I wouldn't have to go back in.

"I can't. I'm too busy trying to hike the ball. And before I'm finished, he smacks me and I'm down. Why doesn't the ref call it?"

When the time-out ended and as play was resuming, Coach looked in my direction. "Kinchlow," he said, "get in there at center."

I trotted out to the ball with as much bravado as I could muster, but I was a bit uncertain. Actually, scared would be a better description. That was a big guy lining up in front of the ball. And I could swear he had a smirk on his face. He knew he was destroying our other center.

We lined up, the signal came, and I snapped the ball. It was on its way, fast and true. I lifted my eyes, and there it came. This fist was headed for my face. We didn't have face guards in those days, and I was ready to get it. But I ducked with all the speed I had. I guess the big guy was a little tired or something and perhaps my reflexes were quicker than my teammate's had been, because he drove his bare fist full force right into the top of my helmet. A violent yell erupted, and he rolled over on his side, clutching his hand. I don't believe it was broken, but it might as well have been. He was wiped out for the rest of the game. I looked over at the sidelines and spit. I was *bad,* man. Nobody better mess with this kid.

The irony of it was that, as I pressed on to carry out my assignment in the play, and just as it ended, another big guy fell across my legs from the back, a clip, and down I went. He landed on my feet and I felt something snap. It was my ankle—broken.

The pain wasn't instantly bad, but I couldn't get up. I kept trying to get to my feet, but I couldn't. And nobody called time-out. I guess they didn't see me, or something, but they ran back to the huddle and began calling the next play. I crawled clumsily to the sidelines and collapsed as the pain set in. Meanwhile, my teammates broke huddle and rushed to the line of scrimmage, and, behold, they had no center. We ended up almost losing that one. We won the game, but they threw rocks at the bus on the way out.

So for the rest of the season, I was in a cast and hobbled around everywhere, falling in more and more with Prez and his boys and the rest of those who hung around the streets of Gunga Din.

* * *

For most of my four years at St. Peter Claver's Academy, I felt a bit alienated from the nuns. I was fascinated by them, and I believe I internally respected them. But there was a wall between us. First, and obviously, they were white and all the students were black. Were they working with us because they wanted to? Or had they got stuck with a bad deal? I was never sure. It seemed to me that few of them were happy. They rarely smiled. And I personally believed they did not like us very much, if at all. I have noted that I picked up on things that many others let roll by. But you can sense when people don't like you.

There was one exception among the sisters, however. She was Sister Mary Boniface—a young woman from Ireland who seemed to be happy all the time. She laughed, she joked, she asked questions, and she did her level best to teach us something. It's trite to say, but she was just plain nice. All of us liked her. Indeed, although the word was not frequently found in our vocabularies, we *loved* her.

"Man," I often observed, "Sister Boniface shouldn't be a nun. She's too good!" I hope the nuns of the world will forgive me for that youthful sentiment, but that's the way I felt. She was a whip, a barrel of fun, and I believe she was one of the few people outside our families who cared about us in a true, wholesome sense.

When I graduated, she wrote in my yearbook: "May God

give you the grace to be all you can be." I did not understand what she meant until I was almost forty years old.

That was quite a wish for those days. I seemed to be slipping from the lofty plateau of early life in Uvalde. I had gone out into the world and had fallen far short in any effort to conquer it. My conduct had deteriorated. My optimism had begun to sour. My insecurity seemed locked into place forever. And life was only beginning.

5

Daddy and Church

WHILE I WAS AWAY AT SCHOOL, my father underwent a radical spiritual conversion. He was born again. He became a Christian, thoroughly committed to Jesus Christ. The change was so complete that he became pastor of our church in Uvalde and served three other congregations as well.

I was amazed. Daddy had been such a swell guy, perfect in every way, I felt. But one time when I came home, he was no longer playing baseball on Sunday mornings. This outstanding athlete, reliable parent, and entertaining companion was spending most of his time in church and related activities. He had been saved! And not just superficially; everything had changed. He meant business with the Lord.

At first I was shocked and a bit disappointed. Daddy, I mused, was as crazy as all the others. But gradually I realized that his new status gave me a new status. I was the preacher's kid, and the title carried a certain amount of respect with the other kids' parents, even if it wasn't deserved. In my case, it wasn't. I was fully bent upon proving that, even if my father was crazy and believed all that stuff, I certainly wasn't crazy. So if other kids acted up some, I had to carry it twice as far to show I was cooler than they. I was no namby-pamby.

Even more important than that, though, was the status my new role gave me with the girls and their mothers. Every mother in the black community wanted her daughter to be involved with the preacher's kid. They figured he was safe and a good influence.

I needed that advantage because, as I've noted, I had had little success with girls up to that point. This was taking its toll on me, too, since acceptance had ever so subtly and steadily become a central drive in my life. And I fully exploited my new status, although I never truly fulfilled the role of Don Juan. I was too much of a jerk to succeed in youthful romances. But I showed off a lot, made a lot of noise, and established that I was not "a religious nut" like my parents.

My mother was already a major figure in the Methodist Church in the black community and when Daddy was converted they together were dominant forces. Daddy began to preach and he was good. He was sound, lively, and concerned. He loved people. It was logical to make him the preacher. The Methodist Church also assigned him to the churches in Del Rio, Pearsall, and Hondo. He would preach the first and third Sundays in Uvalde and Del Rio and the second and fourth in Pearsall and Hondo.

Then there were other places where he was invited to visit from time to time. Most of the time when I was home from school, say for the summer, I would go with him. The preaching had no apparent effect on me. Christianity simply was not real to me. It was mere religion, a practice, a discipline, something you did as part of your social life if you liked it. I steadily was coming to see the people who practiced it as weak, mealy-mouthed, unambitious folks who were kidding themselves into thinking everything was going to come out okay if they sang and prayed and added their amens enough. It was not for me, although I could see real possibilities of influence and power for the preachers and their kids. These suckers needed someone to tell them what to do.

* * *

Unhappily, in the black church in America, there are many preachers who don't believe in God, at least as revealed in the Bible. In fact, there is the well-known story of the man struggling down a row in a cotton field, chopping cotton. The sun was brutal and the temperature was 110 degrees. His back felt broken. Finally, as he reached the end of a row, turned, and gazed back down the next long row in that unending field, he looked up to heaven and cried out: "The sun am so hot and these rows am so long; Lord, I do believe I am called to preach." And he became a preacher.

The bigger metropolitan areas are even more cynical. It's not uncommon to hear some of the black preachers described as "nothing but pretty-boy pimps who play on the sympathies of the little old ladies who are blind to reality." Obviously, this is not true in every black church in America, but it is widespread enough to rank as one of the tragedies among blacks in this country.

There have been prominent examples, but hundreds more at lesser-known levels. Blacks remember, for instance, names like Daddy Grace, Prophet Jones, and Father Divine. In Daddy Grace's case, his flock would make a big event out of constructing a long coat, reaching from his neck to his feet, from money. They would stand him up in front of everyone and put it on him, and ooh and ah and hallelujah all over the place. Quite frankly, Daddy Grace lived like a maharajah off his people. And that was described as Christianity.

Father Divine was well-known across the country for his money-making operations. He sucked in thousands of dollars from poor working people; his schemes had many dimensions. For example, he married a young white woman and began to suggest that he himself was divine—after all, he was called Father Divine—and that she would be the mother of the next messiah. However—and it became complicated—she was too pure to engage in ordinary sexual practices so she would conceive immaculately and bear a savior.

Practices like this steadily deepened my cynicism. But it wasn't confined to the superstar level. Even as a youngster, I was beginning to hear of preachers in street-corner churches, not so much in small towns like Uvalde, but in larger cities like San Antonio, Detroit, Chicago, Harlem, who were driving big cars and living in big houses while they imposed the principle of tithing on their very poor congregations. The tithes were going to only one place—the preachers' pockets. Very little money found its way to the needs of the community.

They would hold two or three services each Sunday, and every service provided two or three offerings; the black churches didn't stop with just one. The preacher could find many causes that required "spontaneous" giving. In addition, the preacher moved around visiting other churches where special offerings would be taken. The host pastor would get up and say something like, "My people, we have this mighty man of God with us today, and we want to bless this man of God." He'd talk right into the consciences of those little elderly ladies. "Now, ladies, we want to bless Brother John, a true man of God." First he would say, "Now, everybody who is going to give $100 come on out of your seat and come right down front." And a few would come down. Then he would say, "Everybody who is going to give $20 come on down front." And so on down, until every penny had been milked. Even at a young age, I had begun to see all this as a money machine.

After I got older, I also learned that other kinds of immorality were not uncommon among this sort of people. The preachers didn't go after only financial rewards; they preyed on ignorant, deluded women for sexual favors, too.

The sad part of it was—and this didn't come clear to me for many years—that the preachers didn't know any better. They did not know what the church, the preaching, the Bible, the plan of salvation, and the life with God were all about. They truly did not know what salvation meant. The prophet Hosea spoke accurately when he said, "My people are destroyed [cut off] for lack of knowledge."[1]

They did not know that Jesus had plainly taught: "Verily, verily, I say unto thee, Except a man be born again, he cannot see the kingdom of God."[2]

They simply did not understand what it meant to be born again. They didn't understand the consequences of man's fall, his spiritual death, and separation from God. Certainly they knew that Jesus had died—even, somehow, that He had died for them. But they hadn't been told that not only must they *believe* that Jesus is the Son of God who died to pay the penalty for their sins, but that they must embrace and receive Him, appropriating this unique mercy and grace into their own personal lives. They hadn't been told they were to accept salvation and follow Jesus as the Lord of their lives.

The preachers didn't understand, and therefore they didn't believe. Their people were the same way. The ordinary folks didn't read the Bible carefully and thoughtfully, often because of their low educational levels, and consequently were subject to error and distortion. Many preachers were little better off. Some of them would find a lady in the congregation, maybe a school teacher, who could read fairly well and they would get her to stand in front of the congregation and read a portion of Scripture. The preacher would follow along behind her, literally. She would read, and he would repeat after her. Then he would come upon a portion that he liked and he would take off on it.

I remember a preacher taking off one time on the seraphim—the celestial beings mentioned in the early vision of the prophet Isaiah. As he was being called to the role of prophet, Isaiah "saw the Lord sitting upon a throne, high and lifted up, and his train filled the temple." Above the throne, he said, were the seraphim. Well, this preacher was captured by the image, not having fully read and understood the passage, and cried out the question, "Now who do you say the seraphim was?" With great dramatic effect and elaboration, he answered his own question, "It was a musical instrument they use in heaven."

Maybe some will say no great harm was done. But the man was mistaken. And if he was wrong in the lesser things, how about the major facts?

Later I realized that most of the black preachers I heard in those days took their sermons from the Old Testament. I assume they figured fewer people in their congregations would know about the Old Testament, and they would be safer if they took off on a passage from there. "My text today is taken from Nehemiah," one would declare. "And it says that 'all the people gathered themselves together as one man into the street that was before the water gate.'[3] Now I want to speak to you for a few minutes about the 'water gate.' We all know how those scoundrels in Washington. . . ." and away he would go.

My point is not to ridicule the uneducated or the poorly trained. The point is that many, many black people were, and still are, deprived of clear preaching of the Word of God. And the Word itself makes plain that preaching is central to helping people find their way to a personal relationship with God. "Faith cometh by hearing," Paul the apostle said, "and hearing by the word of God," thus posing the question, "How shall they hear without a preacher?"[4]

This is heart-breaking. Black people have been a lot like the people of Israel as described by Paul. In a wrenching passage about his own people, he wrote: "Brethren, my heart's desire and prayer to God for Israel is, that they might be saved. For I bear them record that they have a zeal of [for] God, but not according to knowledge."[5]

Black people in general have an undeniable zeal for God. They have suffered so terribly through much of their history and have often had no other recourse but to throw themselves completely on Almighty God. And He looks upon them with great love and compassion. But often their own religious leaders have misled them, just as did so many leaders of Israel as described by Paul and the prophets before him. The Old Testament prophet Jeremiah spoke strong words about the priests and prophets who did such things to the people of God: "Woe be unto the pastors [shepherds] that destroy and scatter the sheep of my pasture! saith the Lord. Therefore thus saith the Lord God of Israel against the pastors that feed my people; Ye have driven them away, and have not visited them: behold, I will visit upon you the evil of your doings, saith the Lord."[6]

Jeremiah continued:

> Mine heart within me is broken because of the prophets; all my bones shake; I am like a man whom wine hath overcome, because of the Lord, and because of the words of his holiness.
>
> For the land is full of adulterers; for because of swearing [cursing] the land mourneth; the pleasant places of the wilderness are dried up, and their course [violence] is evil, and their force is not right.
>
> For both prophet and priest are profane; yea, in my house have I found their wickedness, saith the Lord.[7]

As it was with the Israelites, so it was with blacks, although my young mind did not have any of this worked out through biblical understanding in those days. I merely knew something was wrong. I had detected hypocrisy, and it turned me off, even if my dad, the new preacher, was sincere. Both he and my mom were believers; they had been converted, born again. I accepted that—for them. But I had been disillusioned by what I had seen among most of the people. After all, Mama and Daddy were *supposed* to be good. But what about the others?

To me, a virile if unfulfilled teenager, church was primarily the place to find dumb young girls, just ripe for the plucking. They knew from nothing. Their parents knew from nothing. Mothers even encouraged their daughters to go out with me. The preacher's kid was home free.

* * *

Another reason for my cynicism about the church, and perhaps about my dad's conversion, was the fragmentation I saw among the churches even in a little town like Uvalde. The inability of the local congregations to agree on almost anything caused me to doubt whether there was any concrete truth to the whole Christian message. Maybe they couldn't agree because there really was nothing to agree on. You can push this right into the present day: should we be surprised that so many young people grow up wondering if there is anything solid about the faith? If everybody's got his own "interpretation," maybe there's no substance to the entire matter.

I was that way. In the South, there are white Baptist churches, and there are black Baptist churches; there are white Methodist churches, and there are black Methodist churches and ne'er the twain shall meet. If there is anything truthful in what they are doing, why don't they do it together? That's the way my young mind went—and I wasn't alone.

The African Methodist Episcopal Church was begun because some white Methodists in Philadelphia would not let the black Methodists come to the altar to worship. So the black Methodists pulled out. Drawing some on Methodist practices and some on Episcopal practices, they mixed it with their natural African heritage and founded the AME. The body of Christ was further fragmented.

In Uvalde, as in most other communities across America, the churches would bravely observe Brotherhood Sunday year after year. On that day, a delegation of folks from the white Methodist church, for example, would go down to the black Methodist church for the evening service. All of them would smile a lot and shake hands and act as though they were on the verge of a harmonious breakthrough. The preacher would preach on the brotherhood of believers or some such thing; they would sing loudly together; and then the whites would leave.

That was that, until the next Brotherhood Sunday when a delegation from the black Methodist church would trudge over to the white Methodist church and repeat the process. The only difference was that the blacks usually took several days to get over the plushness of the white church, with its pile carpeting, soft cushions in the pews, magnificent pipe organ, and stained-glass windows. We were used to sawdust or dirt on the floor, benches that wobbled and tilted crazily, and windows with white paint smeared across them to keep people from looking in and laughing.

Such "brotherhood" hypocrisy did not rest well with a young black (or a young white) in the fifties and sixties.

It's amazing that the overall church was as strong in Uvalde as it apparently was. For I remember my mother joking about the disunity, which I found inexplicable among people who contended they knew the truth. "There's the Methodist church right here on this corner," she would say, "and right across the street from it is the Baptist church. And the Methodists are over here singing their spiritual songs at the top of their lungs, 'Will there be any stars in my crown . . .' and right across the street the Baptists are singing, 'No, not one, no, not one. . . .' "

The Baptists didn't like the Methodists. The Methodists didn't like the Episcopalians. The Episcopalians didn't like the Pentecostals. And the Catholics thought all of them were crazy. And that's been the problem with the church as long as I have been aware of it. It was years before I realized the true seriousness of this condition throughout the world. Among the Buddhists, the Moslems, the Communists even, there was unanimity of purpose. They might differ in degree or emphasis, depending upon their position in the world, but their goals were the same. The Moslem sects varied in severity of discipline, but they agreed basically on God (Allah). The Russian Communists and the Chinese Communists disagreed a lot, but they agreed on their god (the state) and the adversary (the United States).

The church, on the other hand, couldn't seem to agree on anything, even the divinity of Christ and the authority of Scripture.

In my cynical, simplistic young mind, I figured out a way to approach the fragmentation. If there was anything to this salvation business, then it was obvious that one should be water-baptized by sprinkling in a Methodist church on Sunday; baptized by immersion in the Baptist church, but on a Saturday to accommodate the Seventh Day Adventists; abstain from meat and go to confession in the Catholic church on Friday; and then celebrate the Lord's Supper at night since it was clear that no one ate "supper" in the morning, as most of the churches tried to do.

This was foolish talk, of course, but it revealed the depth of confusion that Christians presented to a youth in his formative years during one of America's most cynical and wrenching periods.

As for the racial differences, I was becoming even more certain that Christianity was basically a white man's religion. I was increasingly aware that all depictions of Jesus showed Him as a white man. Everybody just assumed that He was white. I did, too. But if He was, why should I think He loved me, as preachers, including my father, were always insisting? Other whites didn't seem to love me especially. And if Jesus was white, and was the Son of God as they insisted, then it followed that His Father—Almighty God—was white, and where did that leave me?

These thoughts were beginning to germinate as I struggled with my life, my parents' lives, and the future. My dad, the one I loved and respected and admired more than any man I'd known, had apparently gone off the deep end. Not only had he been saved, but he also had gone into the ministry. He was still a great guy to be with—still alive and fun—but he was busier than ever and fully preoccupied with thoughts of God, the flock, and the lost. My mother, one of the smartest people I'd encountered, was also fully swept up in her faith. She'd always been among the kindest people in town, and now she and her husband were together on the deepest issues of life and her commitment was stronger than ever.

What was I to make out of all this?

* * *

A relatively insignificant event set the direction for my life in the last year of high school. I returned to Uvalde from the academy one day as the long, hot summer was rolling in. As I was walking down West Main and approaching Park, I saw a new gasoline station that was nearing completion. It was a Humble station, I remember, before the company name was changed to Esso and then to Exxon. It was a big station, sparkling new.

For reasons I'm not sure about, my eye landed on three outside doors. They were restrooms, apparently. I was curious. Why three? No signs had been put up, so my curiosity was unsatisfied for several days. Were they for men, women, and children or what?

As my visit to Uvalde drew to a close, I noticed one day that the restroom signs had been put in place. Three of us were walking together and we crossed the street to get a better look. The carefully lettered signs—black on white—were stark.

"White Men. White Women. Colored."

At that instant, I made up my mind I was not returning to Uvalde after high school. I was not going to live in a town that did that to people.

I'm not sure why that event loomed so large at the moment. Presumably it had to do with my recent immersion in the big-city culture of San Antonio where there were so many black people that all of social life seemed changed. Restaurants, stores, dry cleaners, movies (all owned by whites), everything was located right in the area where you lived, and you were free to come and go as you pleased. You literally were immersed in a black culture and lost sight of the fact that you were black and a lot of other people on the outside were white. White people did not come into your area, except on your terms, and so you didn't have to go to the back of the bus, or sit in the balcony at the movies, or drink from "colored" drinking fountains or seek out segregated restrooms. It was all segregated—all black.

Whatever the cause, I determined right then that when I finished high school I would not come back home to stay. What would happen to me? I wasn't certain. But a distinct seed had been planted inside me. It was distinct, but it carried the aroma of the old insecurity.

6

Escape

IT WAS SUMMER 1955. I joined the U.S. Air Force.

I had made up my mind several months earlier when two recent graduates turned up at St. Peter Claver's Academy wearing Air Force uniforms. They were the sharpest looking dudes I'd seen lately. And the girls went crazy over them. I picked up on that immediately, for I still had not had a meaningful, lasting relationship with any girl. They seemed to *like* me, and we went out together. There were the usual back seat encounters, and several said they actually cared for me. But the old insecurity quirk always seemed to take over, and I thought they were playing games with me, putting me on. I couldn't handle it. So I never had a genuine girl friend.

Anyone who captured the attention of the females, therefore, captured my attention, too. I wanted a touch of what they had.

Furthermore, the Air Force could send you to exotic places, far from Uvalde and its segregated service station restrooms.

When graduation came, my mind was made up.

* * *

I was seventeen years old and determined to pursue a thirty-year career in the Air Force, at minimum. I asked the recruiter if I could sign up for twenty years to begin with.

"No, son, the most you can sign on for is four years," he smiled.

"Okay," I said, "if that's the best you can do, I'll take twenty years, four at a time. What do I do next?"

I signed up and, interestingly, headed back to San Antonio, the site of Lackland Air Force Base. At that time, Lackland and Sampson in New York were the gateways to the Air Force, with virtually all basic training done there.

I arrived at the induction center with a busload of other recruits and as we filed along this endless line of young men— black, white, brown—a sergeant gave us each a serial number.

"Memorize it," he said. "Now. 189789410."

"One, eight, nine, seven, eight, nine, four, one, zero," I repeated. All the way through the line, I kept saying it to myself. I could see the others doing the same thing. Closing their eyes. Squinting. Poking the air with their fingers. Speaking half-aloud.

As I stepped outside, the sergeant said, "You got your serial number memorized?" He was pretty tough.

I straightened up. "Yes, sir. One, eight, nine, seven, eight, nine, four, one, zero."

"Okay," he said, without a trace of friendliness. "Get in line over there."

We all lined up, looking straight into the back of the next guy's head. "If you're taller than the man in front of you, tap him on the shoulder, and move up," the sergeant said. I looked at the one in front of me, and I was at least five inches taller than he was, so I tapped him and stepped in front of him. The same with the next guy. I was taller by far than he was. So I moved up. I kept doing this until finally I was in front of the entire line. I glanced over at the sergeant. He was expressionless.

"All right," he said, looking at me. "From now on, you're the squad leader. You count all the men in your line and make sure they're on the bus when you leave. You're responsible for making sure they show up where they're supposed to be. You're in charge."

I couldn't believe it. I'd only been here a couple of hours, and I was in charge—so what if it was just because I was taller than everyone else. And I wasn't in charge of just the black guys. He had said move up in front of everybody, black *and* white; race hadn't even been mentioned. And I was given two temporary stripes—as fast as that.

Standing there in the sun, bursting with self-esteem and optimism, I thought, *Hey, this is where it's at. This is the life. I've found a home.* As far as I was concerned at that moment, I was in the Air Force for life. This was my country—America. I had always had strong patriotic tendencies to begin with, despite Uvalde restroom incidents and other disturbing moments like that. I would get cold shivers—goose bumps—at the playing of the National Anthem. From my young days at Nicolas Street School, where we took such things seriously, I was most earnest during the recitation of the Pledge of Allegiance.

Some of my enthusiasm had racial overtones, but still blended in with patriotism. Joe Louis, for example, was the greatest of heroes at the time and I became filled with national fervor over him and his long string of victories that stirred blacks all across the land. Jackie Robinson was a great national hero, too. Mix his exploits with the playing of the National Anthem before game time, and I turned into a mass of warm, gushy patriotism.

All of that carried over into the early days of my Air Force career. Basic training was a piece of cake. I was in charge of my group, and I was well liked, and nobody seemed to care that I was dark-skinned. The time passed quickly.

As basic training wound down, I was put through a series of tests and finally offered three career paths—tower operator, member of the Air Police, or communicator. I wasn't sure I liked the idea of bringing airplanes in; the responsibility seemed awesome. And I knew everyone hated cops, including the Air Police. So I settled on a career as a communications specialist. I would learn about telephone switchboards, teletypes, data processing. The communications systems at Air Force installations are massive and complex, ranging from the most primitive to the technologically advanced. Bases had message centers similar to a Western Union office, with the data going and coming in every form, from basic cables to the coded messages handled by the cryptographers. It was busy and at the heart of activities.

It would be a good life. And it had been set in motion simply because nobody seemed to care that I was black, but they were impressed that I was approaching my full adult height and stood six-feet-four. I was still skinny, but starting to fill out a bit as a result of my high school football regimen. Things were going to be okay.

* * *

Having made my communications choice, I was shipped off to Francis E. Warren Air Force Base near Cheyenne, Wyoming—my first visit anywhere in the States outside the South. And not only was Wyoming outside the South, but it was also in the West. It was different.

In a matter of days, I began to feel the difference, subtly. Relationships between blacks and whites were different. Maybe it was because I was only accustomed to the South; maybe it was because it was the West. But blacks seemed less afraid. And yet, being from Uvalde, I hadn't been aware that I was afraid. With hindsight, I see that there is a definite oppression, a subtle heaviness, for blacks, even in communities like Uvalde. It was fear in its root form. Certain kinds of attitudes and a certain treatment were simply accepted. That's the way things were. A white man or woman might do something that insulted or hurt you, but if you recognized it—and many did—you rolled with it. You swallowed the indignity and went about your business. Life had to go on.

That's not the way it was in Wyoming—at least to a large degree. Blacks fought back. They refused to accept the indignities. They did not walk away from conflict. For the first time in my life I saw a black strike a white. I was awestruck. In the South, that was unheard of among black people beyond early childhood.

I remember this guy from Oklahoma. He was a "nice" guy, the kind I'd grown up with in Uvalde. He was one of those whites who didn't seem to know how to say "Negro." The word came out "Nigra" every time, sounding very much like "Nigger." He meant no harm by it; that was merely the way he talked.

A number of us were at the Airman's Club one night—blacks and whites—and Bobby was among us, laughing, kidding, easy-going. At one point he used the word, "Nigra." A slender, quick-moving young black man from Dayton, Ohio, whipped around in the booth and, with an even, low-pitched hardness in his voice, asked, "What did you say, man?" He looked straight into the Oklahoman's merry blue eyes.

"I said Nigra."

Tony's fist flashed out and struck Bobby square on the mouth, knocking his head against the back of the booth. Bobby straightened quickly and blurted out, "What did you hit me in the mouth for?"

Tony's right fist flashed again and hit him in the mouth and Bobby fell out of the booth. After that he got up wiping away the blood and left.

I immediately felt sorry for Bobby. I figured he had meant no harm. His attitude and conduct were simply built right into him. He knew no better. Despite my sympathies for him, however, I grasped the lesson immediately that night. No longer did blacks, at least outside the South, find it necessary to accept just anything whites said or did merely because they were white. That was radical for a young black from Uvalde, Texas.

On another occasion, such a conflict did not end so peacefully. Some of us had dropped in on a dance at the USO Club in downtown Cheyenne. It was a pretty good crowd; the music was good. But there was not an abundance of black women, which was natural for that part of the country.

I watched a black airman approach a white girl not far from where I was standing. I couldn't hear his exact words, but it was obvious that he asked her to dance. I heard her words distinctly. They weren't loud, but I heard each syllable. "I don't dance with niggers."

The airman looked at her for two seconds, although it seemed like an endless time, almost in slow motion. Without a change of expression, he hit her on the mouth. I think it was more of a slap than a punch, but it was a solid blow. "You blankety-blank, rotten, blankety-blank blank."

He wheeled around to storm off the floor and was tackled broadside by a big white airman. In an instant the place erupted, whites fighting blacks, blacks fighting blacks, women against men, women against women. I stood back against the wall and watched. It was chaos—my first race riot, and in Cheyenne, Wyoming, of all places. And the year was only 1956, more than a decade before the revolutionary riots of the late sixties.

The brawl ended when the Air Police arrived, and the crowd dispersed with amazing speed and quietness. I expected everybody to land in jail, but we didn't. My friends and I eased out, went back to the base, and stayed away from the USO for a couple of months.

I soon became aware of another difference between the South and the North at that time. In the South, nobody paid a lot of attention if two blacks disagreed or fought. The authorities felt it was just "those niggers—you know how they are." And if a white man hit a black man, perhaps hurting him badly, or worse, the authorities *might* take action, particularly if the black man died; the offender *might* get thirty days in jail. But if a black man hit a white man—which was rare— he would land in jail for a long time. If the white man died, the black man died.

I was surprised to find that in Wyoming, the law moved with equal force in disputes between blacks and blacks, whites and whites, or blacks and whites. Rightly or wrongly, I tended to think that since there was little economic competition between the races because of the small number of blacks—thus diminishing the fear factor among whites—everyone was treated rather equally.

It was in Cheyenne, however, that I encountered desperate intensity, raw fear, and the disregard for human life that infected some segments of black society. For the first time, I saw safety razor injectors used as weapons.

The first incident happened one evening when I was in the barracks, standing off to one side talking off-handedly with a very short, slender airman from New York City, who was also black. We were joking back and forth, jiving, watching everybody else, and suddenly we were needling one another. He made some remark about my height and size and about the "country boy" from Uvalde, and I immediately said, "Shut up, you little twirp," and something like, "I'll knock your head off." He was a tiny fellow, hardly rising to my shoulder. I was still joking and laughing and thought it was all in fun.

Before I could guess what was happening, I saw his hand slip into his pocket and out again. For some reason that I'm not sure about, as his hand moved from his pants pocket toward me, I instinctively leaned back a fraction of an inch and turned away, my back toward him. The hand made a motion so fast that it was hardly visible and I felt something almost like a shaft of wind down my back. When I craned my neck to look over my shoulder, I could see that my long Air Force blouse was very neatly sliced open for about ten inches. I realized then that the guy was holding a small razor blade dispenser from which he had broken off an injector to expose the menacing edge of the blade. If I had not leaned back, he would have cut me badly, perhaps fatally.

"Hey, man! You're crazy!" I said. "What are you *doing?*"

He simply laughed and slipped his hand back into his pocket. I wasn't prepared to press the argument, and some of the other guys joined us, so we laughed the matter off.

But that airman was crazy, in a sense. He was street crazy. He had fallen into the drive for survival that exceeded anything I had experienced, even on the streets of San Antonio. "Big San Antonio" was still small town after all. That was the fifties, the early beginnings of a fierce struggle that was to sweep America.

* * *

I was unprepared for one social phenomenon I observed in Wyoming. Black men were actually seen dating white women. Maybe there was grumbling among some over this, but for the most part people seemed to ignore it. Where I had come from, it was generally known that white men would go out with black women—not openly, but as we used to say, "messing around." Many black people were offended by this, but nothing was said. That was just the way it was.

In Cheyenne, black men dared to step across that line and were seen in public places with white women, dancing, eating, talking seriously.

All of this was important to a young black man, considering that everything around him works to convince him that the most desirable thing in the world is to have money, a big car, and a white woman. Magazines, television—almost all forms of advertising—condition the black to think of these as the ultimate achievements. Some of that has been changing in the last twenty years, but it's still there underneath. A white woman, especially a blonde, was the epitome of success. A black man had arrived if he could drive up to a place in a Cadillac and walk inside with a woman like that on his arm.

I did not have that kind of success in Wyoming. I danced with two or three white women, enough to learn they smelled different, but I never had a white girl friend. In fact, that bothered me some. There must be something wrong with me. Why wasn't I scoring like the rest of the guys?

* * *

In the early months of my Air Force career, the creeping insecurity that had haunted me since childhood seemed to develop into a minor disorientation, a kind of internal loneliness. With reflection, I realized that I had lived in a Roman Catholic context for four years. I had gone to mass regularly, I had been ruled and instructed by nuns, and despite the fact that such religious life seemed to have no internal effect on me, I felt somewhat estranged once I had left it behind. I believe I felt a deep desire to *belong* to something.

So, at the end of basic training, I went back to San Antonio and joined the Catholic Church. I went through several talks with a priest, then baptism, confirmation, and first communion.

And for the next several months, I went to mass every Sunday so that whenever I could get liberty, I had a place and friends to go to in San Antonio. I *belonged* to something. I have no recollection that this was an especially meaningful experience for me internally. I was not acting from a point of faith. I did not have peace with God, for example; indeed, I thought very little about God. He was far off somewhere, if He existed at all.

But at least I had some common ground with some other folks. I was not completely alone.

* * *

My first assignment after Communications School was in Labrador. I was sent to the top of the world, Saglak, where

135 of us lived in an inverted icebox, designed to keep the cold out rather than in. We lived twelve months inside that huge, inside-out refrigerator. It was our working quarters, living quarters, eating quarters, recreation quarters—everything. There was no place else to go. I went outside once, maybe twice, during the twelve months I was there. Believe me, it was cold.

Our installation, which was for aircraft control and early warning—part of the Distant Early Warning Line, or "DEW Line"—sat high on a rock overlooking Baffin Bay. Nothing blocked the view from our huge radome with its radar antennae pointed over the North Pole toward the Soviet Union. The only way to get up on that rock was with those remarkably agile vehicles called snowcats. They took us from a lower camp up to the top of the rock and left us. There was no way to get down.

Near the end of what was called summer—late August or early September—I went outside. Some of the rocks were bare, but still a layer of snow covered most of the terrain. The wind was fierce, blowing above seventy miles an hour that day; usually it was ninety or a hundred. I had never felt anything like it. As I bent low and trudged back into the building, I understood how isolated I really was. There would be no way to survive for more than a few minutes outside that massive icebox. We were alone at the top of the world. Very few knew we were there; very few cared.

* * *

I worked. I sat behind my desk, mostly waiting. Nothing ever happened, but I dreaded that something would, because it would mean big trouble. Like World War III. Occasionally an encrypted message would come in and my heart would start pounding. Then we'd decrypt it, I'd relax, and distribute it appropriately. Most often it was nothing more than the location of some B-52's or tankers. Then I'd settle in to wait some more.

I ate. The food was good, and we ate in shifts, around the clock. I actually never knew what time of day it was; my watch showed a number, but it meant nothing inside that monstrous igloo. There were few windows. I simply ate when the number said it was time. That's the way we did everything.

But I had everything I wanted to eat—steak, chicken, milk, cake, ice cream.

I read. My lifelong habit of devouring everything in sight was fed to the fullest in Labrador. Paperbacks, magazines; science fiction, adventure; politics, philosophy, history—I read it all. Some I retained; a lot I lost immediately. But it was a significant time. The world was yielding its secrets to me.

I watched movies. The Air Force did everything it could to keep us well supplied with fairly current films along with a lot of old ones. And they played endlessly.

Most significantly, I drank. Liquor became a regular part of life during this period. It was the center of my existence for twelve months. We could buy the best whiskey on the market for ten or fifteen cents a shot. Twenty-five cents bought a double eight-year-old scotch, and that was my mainstay. Beer was ten cents a can, if you wanted it; I never became much interested in it. But I liked the scotch. Or rather, I liked the feeling it produced. I don't believe I drank because I liked the taste of it. I drank to "feel good." It did wonders for insecurity—until it wore off, and then the estrangement and loneliness were worse than ever. Hangovers carry desperate insecurity.

I recall arriving at Saglak in the howling wind, grateful to be inside after the treacherous trek up there by snowcat. After checking into my room—we all had our own, without a hint of segregation—I followed the others to the bar. Impressed with the bargain prices, I went for straight scotch. Buying the best booze in the world did something for morale. I was on my own. No T.I., no bed check—free at last.

I looked around at my comrades and felt that warm feeling of fellowship. It was the scotch, of course. But these were my colleagues, and we were doing something important. We were patriotic young Americans, and we were making a sacrifice. And we were together.

The scotch helped maintain that feeling every day. Now and then, I shifted to bourbon. But I really didn't like the taste, so I added a touch of ginger ale or Coke. I tasted brandy, too, and it wasn't bad. But scotch was the mainstay, and it worked quickly—sometimes much too quickly.

The scotch seemed to supplant my enthusiasm and my need for religion. My new-found Catholicism produced very little activity in Labrador. I attended mass two or three times and then let it dwindle to attending only on major holidays. Perhaps the closeness of life with 135 men met the need my religion had supplied; perhaps it was the drinking. Probably the cause lay in the fact that my burst of ardor for church was mainly an external reaction to insecurity and produced very little internal change.

I really had not found a relationship with God. I didn't know biblical language and certainly not theology, but unquestionably a chasm existed between God and me. It was a chasm of darkness. I couldn't see across it. And I wasn't sure God was actually on the other side of the chasm. I wasn't sure anything was there. I was sure only that I was here. And I was sure of the darkness. Those two certainties married and begat an oversized offspring that lived within me.

I have referred to that offspring as insecurity. And that's as good a name as any. It is a deep, gnawing fear that must eventually disguise itself because men do not like to acknowledge fear in themselves. It must take on hardness if it's to survive. The hardness can take the form of further withdrawal into absolute independence, extreme individualism, perhaps eccentricity, that warps and worsens with age. Or the hardness can move toward anger, hatred, meanness, and total disregard for everyone and anything.

Both directions actually point the same way—to total selfishness. I wasn't sure which of those directions I was heading —withdrawal or anger. I believe the decision hung in the balance during those early Air Force days.

Could I possibly bridge that dark chasm? Did I dare?

7

The Turn Begins

SHREVEPORT, LOUISIANA. I'll never forget it.

Several weeks had passed, and I needed a haircut. I hadn't found my way around Barksdale Air Force Base and the local community yet, so I headed for the most logical place, the PX.

It was like most Post Exchanges, big, low-ceilinged, brightly lighted, and jammed full of everything any Air Force family could need. I spotted a sign and passed through the main PX into an attached room, which was a barbershop. One glance showed there wasn't a black man in the place. It was for whites only—on a USAF base in the continental United States! I could see another room beyond it, so I kept walking and passed through into a second barbershop—for blacks.

I had never been segregated since joining the Air Force, and I was astounded. How could this be? The thought slipped into my mind as I took off my jacket and waited my turn.

"You're back in the Deep South, baby." A cold loneliness—isolation—formed like a solid mass in my chest. It grew and grew, pressing outward. And it forced itself up into my throat. I thought I would gag. Was this the way it was? Forever?

I was twenty-one years old. I had left my home, trying to break out of the feelings of separation and inferiority that had begun to creep over me in Uvalde, epitomized by the segregated restroom facilities at the new service station. But here I was. Right back in the middle of it—only worse.

Why was it bothering me so? I wasn't sure, myself. I guess it was symbolic to me. It was a bigger wedge, the kind that kept trying to drive me into a corner, a corner where voices whispered, "You are different . . . you don't belong . . . you're not as good as everyone else . . . nobody cares anything about you." I was afraid of that corner. I was afraid that I really was different, that I was inadequate, that I might find out I would never belong anywhere.

So I did what most of the other blacks did. I headed for a place to congregate. In San Antonio, it had been Gunga Din and East Commerce. In Shreveport, it was "The Bottoms," down on the Red River bank. The nightclubs were down there. So were the pimps, the whores, the addicts, the drunks. Anything you wanted, you could get there. It was the place to hang out.

One night four of us went down there and got pretty high. We were feeling no pain, just lolly-gagging along, laughing and whooping it up. Just before we crossed over to the downtown area, we found a coffee shop, had something to eat, and decided to return to the base.

We were still pretty tipsy while waiting for the public service bus, but were causing no trouble. We were just a bit loud. I swung up onto the bus first, still laughing and horsing around, and after I dropped my money into the slot, without thinking, I flopped into the first empty seat. The other guys boarded the bus and walked toward the rear and I continued laughing and hollering back to them. I thought it was odd that they all of a sudden didn't seem to be having as much fun as I was.

Suddenly, I realized that the bus had gotten extremely quiet. I looked up, and everybody seemed frozen. They all looked straight at me. I turned toward the bus driver, and he didn't move. He was looking in the rearview mirror. He was staring at me.

What's the matter? I thought. *What's he looking at?*

His hand was merely resting on the gearshift knob. It was not moving. He looked at me. Was he mad, or afraid, or maybe sick?

Then it dawned on me. I was on the wrong end of the

bus. Everybody was waiting to see what I was going to do. Was I going to start something? Was there going to be a riot? Inadvertently I had just staged perhaps the first civil rights demonstration in America, an activity Rosa Parks would bring to national prominence in the sixties.

With every bit of laughter drained from me, I looked into the mirror at the driver's face for just a second. I looked at the floor. Then I pulled myself up with one hand on the metal floor pole beside me and crossed the white line painted on the floor.

I felt the gear slip into place, and the bus moved forward easily. I had assumed my proper place. The tension burst, and a low hubbub of conversation resumed. Somehow I didn't feel like laughing anymore.

The next morning I went to squadron headquarters and filed a request for transfer. I didn't care where I went. I wanted out of the South.

* * *

While I waited for a transfer, I spent most of my free evenings in The Bottoms and soon after the bus incident, I ran straight into the meanness and disregard for human life that is always near the surface of so much of street life. Again, it was a bar. I was sitting talking to a hooker. The conversation was nothing extraordinary, but I was kidding around, treating her rather coarsely but with good humor. I didn't know any better.

I called her a foul name. "You little blankety-blank. I ought to teach you a lesson. I ought to reach over there and knock your head off." I thought I was pretty cool.

She let a trace of a smile flicker on her lips as she gently waved a brightly colored handkerchief across her mouth. She looked hard into my eyes. I laughed, and half raised my fist.

With the handkerchief in her hand she casually reached toward me, and flipped it across my neck. I was sitting quite close to her in the dark smoky haze of the barroom. "I ought to bash you," I said again, with a silly smile. With that, she flicked the handkerchief again and let it fall open. My eyes dropped to it, and there within its folds lay a naked razor blade.

My mouth went dry, and the muscles in my throat tightened. It would have been as easy for her to cut my throat with a twist of the wrist as it was for her to flick the handkerchief across my face. I would never have seen the blade.

She merely stared into my face. Her pretty lips parted ever so slightly in a trace of a smile; her white teeth glistened. Not a hint of human compassion, concern, or emotion showed in her eyes. Nothing. Life was survival—at any cost. Death meant little. I could have bled out my life on a filthy bar room floor, another statistic: "Black airman killed in bar. Hooker out on bail the following day."

I had to get out of there. I had to find a place where I could live, not just exist.

* * *

French Morocco was the immediate answer. I was transferred to Sidi Slimane Air Force Base about forty miles from Rabat. It was a Strategic Air Command base, a good assignment.

As a romanticist and an avid reader, I was swept up in the imagined glamor of Morocco itself and wasted little time before exploring places like Casablanca and Marrakesh. My mind was a jumble of Arabian Nights and the French Foreign Legion.

Of course, the Moroccan houses of ill repute, the narrow streets, the smoke-filled rooms, the dimmed lights, the dangling beads, the belly dancers—everything had to be tasted. I made the rounds with four or five buddies. I remember the thrill of passing through those mysterious dangling beads and going into the depths of one of the notorious houses. It was romantic for the first few hours, but then the dirt and decadence—the fight for survival—seeped through the veneer of romance. Night life in Morocco was as ugly as it had been in Louisiana.

Eventually I was struck with how poorly we blacks treated the Moroccans. Although blacks and whites were thoroughly integrated in our work lives, blacks usually traveled together as we socialized, and strangely enough, we treated the Moroccans as shabbily as we were treated at home by the whites. We were rude to the Moroccan women; we showed no respect for anyone. I came to understand that the reputation, "Ugly American," could apply to black Americans as well as to white.

I recognized a certain irony in all this. In quiet moments, the moral principles I had grown up with rose to the surface and confronted the immorality and meanness I was seeing around me. The disregard for people—the disregard for life— troubled me. Unfortunately, and yet naturally, I was concerned mainly about how all this affected me. I watched others get hurt, but my thoughts really flowed to concern about how I might ultimately be affected. Was this disregard, this callousness, going to take hold of me?

At this point, I wasn't mean. Indeed, most people thought I was a nice guy. But I was a conniver. I had a great facade. I knew how to maneuver; I could outwit most of my peers. For instance, if I saw a fight developing, I knew how to stay clear. To me, fighting was the last resort for people unable to think or talk their way out of a problem. If I fought, there could be no stopping, even if the opponent gave up. There was always the possibility that he might come back another day and do me in. No, as far as I was concerned, if you were going to fight, then take it to its ultimate conclusion, which meant someone was likely to get killed.

In retrospect, I guess God was keeping me out of trouble for His purposes, so I didn't get in a lot of fights in those days. I simply let "the dumb, ignorant masses" beat up on one another. Maybe I was getting pretty arrogant deep down inside.

I thought I was concerned with the "deeper things" of life. Indeed, I felt I was a pretty deep dude. I saw myself as thoughtful and imaginative. But in fact, I was running at a very shallow level. All I really cared about was me. Because of my upbringing, I was always aware of certain moral principles. I knew there was a right and a wrong. But I hadn't paid much attention to why that was so. I figured I was calling the shots myself. I didn't think about God very often; He wasn't particularly relevant, it seemed. A mass here, a confession there, a prayer when you were in a bind—that was it, at best. Other than that, I did what I pleased. These moral principles didn't keep me from doing anything I really felt like doing. But self-indulgence isn't particularly satisfying either.

As a result, I was unhappy most of the time—never more than half-fulfilled. When I was alone I was quiet, often moody; publicly I tried to be bright-eyed and jolly, but I was often pensive, doubtful about the future. I began to equate this periodic sadness, this quiet discontent, with intelligence and thoughtfulness. I was vain enough to think that I was smart, that since I knew more than everyone else, I was therefore beyond genuine happiness. If you were smart, I reasoned— if you really knew the score—then you had to be unhappy.

Anyone who had spent as much time in church as I had— albeit under duress—had somewhere heard something on the "fullness of life." But it had never sunk in that those things were really for people—today, now. Somehow I had always thought that the things of the Bible were for sometime, somewhere way down there in the future, "in the sweet by and by."

I knew I didn't have "fullness of life," but I didn't think anybody else did, either. That's why I could kid myself into thinking I was a spiritual guy. Yet Paul the apostle had written in the Bible that "the fruit of the Spirit is love, joy, peace, longsuffering, gentleness, goodness, faith, meekness, temperance."[1]

Love, joy, peace? They were just words. Who knew anyone who was genuinely loving, joyful, and peaceful? Longsuffering and patient? Gentle? Meek? Those were the characteristics of a doormat, it seemed to me. That would be the guy who would get nowhere. Yet Paul said they were the marks of happiness, the marks of strength. "Against such there is no law," he said. How could that be?

I hadn't read far enough in the Bible on my own to see that the external principles themselves weren't enough. It talked about some "internal dimension" that I wasn't ready for at the moment. It talked about being "crucified with Christ," something deep down inside, something genuinely "spiritual," unlike the common usages of that term in our day.

In talking about the fruit of the Spirit, Paul said, "and they that are Christ's have crucified the flesh with the affections and lusts."[2] That was far deeper than my shallow, self-centered concerns. They did not begin to approach his suggestions for true happiness: "If we live in the Spirit, let us also walk in the Spirit. Let us not be desirous of vain glory, provoking one another, envying one another."[3]

I was missing life. But I didn't know it as I bounced from one thing to another.

* * *

In Morocco, I began to play basketball for the Air Force. First I played in the squadron league and then moved up to play for the base team. Having attained most of my height and put on some weight in Labrador, I was rangy and quick—a natural jock, as they say.

It was pretty good ball and it opened a lot of doors for me. With it came a certain notoriety. Everyone recognized me and wherever I went there was at least a superficial friendship—a lot of "Hey, what's happening, Kinch?" and that sort of thing. Jocks are in something of a spotlight, and that was better than being ignored.

The main benefit of my ball-playing was travel. We moved all over the region, playing other service teams. The team was fully integrated, blacks and whites, and that was good. Nonetheless, during moments of pure fellowship and socializing, blacks hung with blacks and whites with whites. Maybe it was a matter of security. We felt at ease with our own jiving and lolly-gagging. That's the way we had grown up, and the habit would require a long time to break.

Furthermore, I still remembered the South. The Louisiana barbershop and bus experiences, the service station restrooms in Uvalde and a hundred others were alive in my mind. Maybe I could play ball with the white guys, traveling with them to exotic places I had only dreamed about—Marrakesh, Morocco, Casablanca—but could I ever trust them? That they should ever trust me never occurred to me.

A far deeper question dogged my days and haunted my nights. Was there indeed something different between blacks and whites beyond color and physical make-up? Was there something internally different? Were blacks somehow really inferior, as had been subtly hinted for years? "Separate but equal" was for our benefit we'd been told. We couldn't keep up, they said. I had come to accept the notion, at least emotionally if not intellectually, that maybe there were some things I simply was not able to do. I wasn't exactly sure why. But that's the way it seemed to be.

Later, I began to see we had accepted what we'd been told over and over. Blacks were inferior, second rate, genetically and biologically. Whites said it and gradually blacks began to believe it. Tell someone a thing long enough and it becomes a fact.

I was different. Maybe I was inferior.

How was I to live this out?

* * *

Life was churning inside me, and I didn't like it. I couldn't find anything to grab onto that didn't eventually twist and squirm and elude me. Nothing was solid in my life. I merely bounced from one white man's whim to another, it seemed to me. I was always reacting to someone else's authority. I had no course of my own.

With hindsight, I see that my existence had no real foundation. I actually was adrift. I desperately needed stability in life. It would be many years before I would allow the truth to penetrate my rock-hard skull, but I know I had heard sermons preached on the importance of founding our lives on the rock and not on sand. As Jesus said, "Whosoever heareth these sayings of mine, and doeth them, I will liken him unto a wise man, which built his house upon a rock: And the rain descended, and the floods came, and the winds blew, and beat upon that house; and it fell not: for it was founded upon a rock."[4] But at this point, these were just more words in a sea of words.

We need to do more than *hear* Christ's words. We need to *do* them if we are going to maintain a true course in the raging and buffeting that is going on all around us. The social turmoil that would shake America so violently in the sixties was swelling within the chests of young men and women like myself even in those relatively calm years of the fifties. And I had no foundation. The winds were blowing, and the floods were on their way, and I was beginning to shake.

I didn't recognize it, but my heart yearned to know the meaning of the apostle Paul's teaching about genuine brotherhood, not the kind I had been exposed to in the hypocrisy of so many churches. "For ye are all the children of God by faith in Christ Jesus. For as many of you as have been baptized into Christ have put on Christ. There is neither Jew nor Greek, there is neither bond nor free, there is neither male nor female: for ye are all one in Christ Jesus. And if ye be Christ's, then are ye Abraham's seed, and heirs according to the promise."[5]

This is true equality. Jews, Greeks, Americans, Moroccans, blacks, whites, Hispanics, men, women, children—we are equal before Almighty God if we have placed our faith in Jesus Christ, who is the rock upon which He said we are to build our houses. We can all be one.

Equality and stability. They were eluding me in French Morocco, and they were eluding thousands more like me all over the world. Strife seemed to be our portion. And it was just beginning.

8

Vivian

AFTER MOROCCO, IT WAS BACK TO TEXAS. I had wanted
to stay out of the South, but then this wasn't the Deep South.
This was Texas—home.

It was Saturday night. The weather was warm and pleasant,
a perfect fall evening. I was putting the finishing touches on
my outfit, ready to do something—party, "boot it up"—I just
hadn't decided where. One of the troops occupying a room
in the transient barracks with me, was getting dressed, too.
I had never seen him before and knew nothing about him.
"Hey, brother," he asked, "What you gonna do tonight?"

"I don't know yet," I replied. "I just got here. Going downtown to check out what's happening. What about you?"

"You got wheels?" he asked.

"Yeah, I got a shart. Why don't we ride?"

"Great." He got up off the bed and grabbed his jacket.

My "shart" was a 1957 pink and white Ford Galaxie, perfect
for the mission. Its twin exhausts let off a deep, throaty gurgle
reminiscent of the old PT boats—a muffled, fiercely restrained
rumble ready to explode into action. I had a heavy foot when
driving, but this was cruising time where you roll down the
window, stick out an elbow, lean way over toward the center
of the car, and roll along slowly, letting the engine gurgle
and the radio "cook." Every now and then it was necessary

to burn a little rubber to show the street rods that those pipes were for real.

When I had been in Morocco, and my accumulating money was burning a hole in my pocket, I had taken out an allotment and told my dad to buy me a 1957 Ford. He had bought one—black yet, six cylinder with overdrive. He had to be kidding. . . . When I got back, I didn't like it at *all*, man! It was definitely not a shart, so I had him buy another—the pink and white one. He kept the first.

So my new acquaintance and I headed forth. Right outside the gate we spotted a liquor store and pulled in. "Look, Bro," I said, "it's only seven o'clock. Why don't we get a pint and go back to the room and get mellow—kill a little time? Things won't start jumping downtown until about nine."

"That's cool," he agreed.

"After that we can pick up another one on the way down, and we can stir up a little action."

He nodded approval.

After sipping on the pint for nearly an hour, rambling all over the lot with Air Force yarns and sex stories, most of them fabricated, we set out again.

We were driving through the base toward the service club, cruising appropriately in the pink and white Ford, when I spotted two women crossing the street up ahead. One of them had red hair. I had been in French Morocco for a long time where the women were all covered up all the time, and these two were especially attractive to me. The one with the red hair was really pretty.

"Man, look at that," I said, keeping my eyes on her. "You see that one with the red hair? That's mine. I'm going to get that one."

Somehow I knew I was going to get next to that woman. Something in me locked into place. I was determined.

I slowed the car to a crawl, watching them. They were headed toward the movie theater. I eased over to the side of the street and finally stopped. They went into the movies and I sat staring at the front of the building. A minute passed.

My buddy broke into my thoughts. "Hey, Kinch, let's go!"

Still watching the theater and reaching toward the door

handle, I threw over my shoulder, "Sure, let's go downtown, but wait just a minute while I go over here."

Before he could answer, I was out of the car and cut across the street. "An hour and fifty minutes," the ticket lady said. The movie would let out in an hour and fifty minutes. I darted back across the street, started the engine, and we headed downtown.

We cruised an hour or so, checking out clubs, with virtually no action, and I eventually pulled in to the curb. "Listen, man, I'll see you later. I got to get back before this movie lets out and pick up this chick."

He shook his head and gave me a wry smile. "Okay, Kinch, but I bet you strike out."

I laughed.

I was back in front of the theater with five minutes to spare and I watched from across the street. I wanted a good wide-angle view.

"There she is." My voice was just a whisper. She was a striking black woman, laughing, obviously confident. And her hair was red. Unusual. She looked very good.

"That's mine," I said again with a confidence that had been slow in developing for me.

The redhead and her companion walked quickly into the service club while I plotted my strategy. I parked the car properly and went into the club as quickly as I could. I didn't want to lose them.

There she was—at the snack counter. She was ordering something.

"I wonder what her name is," I said to myself.

An airman walked by the counter. "Hey, Vivian, what's happening?"

She gave him a dazzling smile. I'd never seen such white teeth. I couldn't hear her reply.

"Vivian. Now I know her name."

She took something in a sack from the counterman, said a few words, and then headed out of the club by herself. Her girlfriend stayed behind.

Outside she crossed the patio and headed across the quadrangle toward the barracks. I waited until I got out from under the club lights so she couldn't see me clearly and I called out calmly and steadily in a slightly muffled voice, "Hey, Vivian, wait up."

She slowed her pace and looked back. My mind was racing, but I sauntered toward her, "pimping"—walking my best street walk. "Hey, baby, what's happening?" Profound!

"Not much," she said. She seemed friendly enough. I believe she thought she knew me from somewhere. She still couldn't see me clearly.

"Where are you going?"

"Back to the barracks."

Yes, she was friendly. "What you got there?"

"A cheeseburger."

"Great. Give me a bite."

And, oddly enough, she opened the bag, took out the cheeseburger, and held it out to me, a stranger she didn't know from Cootie Brown. I took a big bite.

Three months later we were married.

* * *

On January 16—the day after payday—we became man and wife before a small gathering of friends, mostly hers, in the main chapel at Carswell Air Force Base. In three months we had run around a lot with the people she had come to know. I had not been there long enough to have a lot of friends.

I didn't even own a suit, so I had to borrow one to get married in. She bought herself a new outfit, but we had to wait until payday because I had used up all my money buying cars. Vivian had some savings, but I had nothing really. I even borrowed the shirt and tie I wore that day.

Our apartment in a place strangely named Stop Six wasn't ready, so we spent our honeymoon weekend in a friend's bedroom in the same apartment complex. The bed broke down as we climbed in.

I was twenty-three years old, and Vivian was twenty-one. She stayed in the Air Force only a few more days and applied for a discharge, which came through handily. I was glad to see her get out because she outranked me.

I was coming up for discharge, unsure about the future, so Vivian and I agreed she should visit her parents till the issue was settled. When I put her on the train I could feel the tears hot in my eyes, so I turned quickly and walked away.

I re-enlisted in a few months and was assigned to Stewart Air Force Base in Newburgh, New York. We immediately learned we could not afford the high cost of apartments in that area, so we arranged for Vivian to keep on living with her mother and father in Newark, New Jersey, about an hour from Newburgh. That was her home, but it was a strange place to me.

I remember driving through Newark for the first time. It was my first experience in a major northern metropolitan area. I was stunned by its size, to begin with. San Antonio had been impressive, but it was a small country town compared with this. Black people in Newark were street smart to the Nth degree. In the ghetto, a man's life meant little; some people would kill for a dime. The casual violence exceeded anything I'd seen in Texas, Wyoming, and Morocco. Killings often were not significant enough even to be recorded in the newspapers.

My wife's parents did not live in the ghetto itself but in an integrated section in a typical row of brownstone houses. People mowed tiny yards, sat outside on the streets in hot weather, and hung out the windows to talk back and forth. You could hear everything that was going on. The noise—the blaring radios, the yelling back and forth, the kids playing hopscotch and stickball on the street—was unsettling for me. After just one day there with Vivian I was tense and anxious.

"Can I keep up with these people?" I wondered. "They're tougher and smarter by far than I am."

The old insecurity rose in my mind before the first weekend had passed. True, I was out of the South, but I was into something I hadn't bargained for. I wasn't sure I could handle it.

* * *

I was surprised to find that the northern cities like Newark had a more rigid segregation in day-to-day living than the areas I'd experienced in the South. I'd been accustomed to life between blacks and whites that was intertwined. Yes, they went to separate schools, used different restrooms, drank from different water fountains, but they lived in the same vicinity.

In many sections of Uvalde, for instance, blacks and whites lived across the street from one another. Even in most parts of San Antonio at that time, many neighborhoods had a mixture of races, cultures, and backgrounds.

This was not so in the northern cities. The races went to school together, but everything else, it seemed, stayed in its own little pocket. Italians lived in one pocket, Jews in another, the Irish in another, and the blacks were separate from all. There was very little intercourse between them. It looked to me as if everybody was discontented.

I wasn't aware of any distinct racial rumblings at that time, just a general malaise. Black people blamed "Mr. Charlie"— the white man—for everything that was wrong. But in 1959 I personally saw no real indications that an uprising was on its way. Black people were merely grumbling about their second-class citizenship the way they had been doing for a hundred years. I must admit, however, that in Newark there was a sharp edge to that grumbling—a definition, a solidity that was new to me.

I spent the weekends in Newark, and the times were tough, financially and otherwise. It was no way to begin a marriage. Usually I would return to Newburgh with just enough money in my pocket to pay the forty-cent toll on the Garden State Parkway.

I remember one Sunday night in particular. I had just left the parkway and was headed down another highway. I must have still been in New Jersey because I can remember the signs, "Speeders Lose Licenses." It seemed to me they were everywhere in New Jersey. Unexpectedly I came upon a police radar trap and a hot flash surged through my body in that second of uncertainty before my eyes could drop to the speedometer. As the cold sweat started to form, I saw that I was doing only 57 miles an hour. I would be okay.

Wrong. A police car pulled in behind me and the man inside waved me over. The officer made all the customary moves about license, registration, and the like and then said, "You were doing 57 miles an hour in a 55 zone."

I couldn't believe it. He was nailing me for exceeding the speed limit by two miles an hour. He explained that the fine was fixed—I believe it was $32.50 and that I would have to pay right then.

"I don't have the money," I told him.

He looked straight into my face. "I'm sorry, but you will have to go to jail." The words were courteous, but the voice was completely detached.

I still couldn't believe this was happening. "Aw, man, if you take me to jail, I'm going to miss roll call and get busted." I was in civilian clothes, so the remark was the first indication I was a serviceman. The younger partner of the officer doing the talking to that point then leaned forward and looked at me. He apparently had recently been in the service.

"Can you prove you're in the Air Force?" he asked.

"Yeah, I got my ID card."

He looked at it, and then asked to look in the trunk of my car. When I opened it, there was an Air Force overcoat. The younger officer said something I missed, and then the first one said, "Well, I'll tell you what. We're going to let you go. As soon as you get back, you mail your money to this address. If you don't. . . ." The implied threat was enough. I would send the money.

I was off the hook. I drove cautiously back to Stewart Air Force Base, borrowed the money, and sent it back to the justice of the peace quickly. But that grounded me for thirty days. My license to drive in Jersey was revoked, and our finances were so tight that I was unable to afford the $1.20 plus gas to Newark and back.

I don't believe race played a part in that episode, but I am certain it was one of those set-ups for the local justice of the peace that are common around the country. They grab a violator and force him to pay on the spot or go to jail, even for 57 miles an hour in a 55 zone. It was not crooked, but it pushed the letter of the law to extremes and added some money to local coffers.

* * *

I began to have doubts about marriage. Vivian and I were separated most of the time, and when we were together we were increasingly testy with one another. I was broke all the time. Had I made a mistake?

Compounding my reservations was the difference between Vivian's family and my own. My mom and dad and their nearby relatives were simple country people basically, which meant they were open and free with one another. They were naïve, far from perfect with plenty of problems, and yet they seemed innocent and generous, friendly.

Vivian's relatives were city people. I believe that was the primary difference. Trust and friendliness were guarded, held back. Too much openness was dangerous in a city like Newark. I didn't sense the close relationships between members of the family the way I had experienced them in Uvalde. Frankly, I felt a strong degree of self-concern among them. It was as though they had to watch out for themselves, and only themselves, all the time. Perhaps survival in such an environment made that necessary.

I remember a small example that registered very clearly with me. It was my first weekend away from Stewart with Vivian in Newark. I went to the refrigerator to pour a glass of milk from a big carton there. Vivian saw me and said quickly, "You can't take that. You have to use ours." I looked at her blankly.

"You have to use ours," she repeated. "That one belongs to Mom."

I learned quickly that we kept our own orange juice, our own lunch meat, our own milk, everything. There was no sharing. What was theirs was theirs; what was ours was ours.

Very gradually I began to feel isolated. I seemed to sense a great difference between myself and those around me, especially Vivian's parents. They didn't like me, I was convinced. I felt they merely tolerated me. Soon this filtered into my own marriage, and I felt unappreciated, as if they thought I was "country." Later on I found this was not the case.

Once a person begins to think that way, he looks around for someone who will appreciate him, someone who will "understand." I needed someone to see what a "nice guy" I was and what a "raw deal" I was getting.

So back at Stewart Air Force Base I started hanging out with the fellows at the bar and the club and talking long hours about what I perceived as a bad situation. I even began to pay some attention to other ladies I occasionally met, nothing serious but more on the order of checking the greener grass on the other side of the fence. I needed to know if everyone was as unhappy as I was becoming.

Even in the times when we were together, Vivian and I were deteriorating into arguments and real quarrels. Our living arrangements were bad. She was pregnant now and felt sick a lot of the mornings while I was there. The weeklong separations were damaging. A new marriage between two young people as different in background and orientation as we were needed a solid, stable environment and some peaceful, quiet times of just plain young romance and love. We didn't have that in Newark.

I believe Vivian and I both inwardly yearned for that stability, and right after our son, Nigel, was born we did scrape together enough to take a small apartment over a department store in Newburgh, New York. Typical of the ease of living it offered was the refrigerator. The kitchen was so small and poorly laid out that the refrigerator door wouldn't open all the way before bumping into the cabinets opposite it. If you wanted to put something in or take it out, you had to angle yourself and the object in such a way as to slide it in. You never could really fill up the refrigerator. It was crazy. And we had to share a bathroom with a couple down the hall. But we were together, and remained so for more than a year, seeming to grow some in our relationship, although the struggle was difficult financially.

Soon, however, word came that I was being transferred to Saudi Arabia, and we had to make new plans. The first thing we did was give up the apartment, and Vivian moved back to her family's home in Newark. I waited for final orders.

* * *

One Friday afternoon I walked into my in-laws' house after a difficult week at Stewart to start a leave the week prior to shipping overseas, and found a strange man sitting in the living room talking to my wife.

What is this? I thought.

Vivian quite calmly introduced the man as one of her "friend boys."

Friend boy? I thought. *What's a friend boy?*

It turned out that this was a fairly common expression in the inner city. It apparently was used to distinguish between "friends" and "boy friends." They both sounded the same to me.

Anger, jealousy, and hostility surged into my chest and throat, and I wasn't overly civil. The man got no conventional courtesy from me, and I blurted out some rather direct criticism.

"You don't need 'friend boys' any more, Vivian," I said. "You're a married woman now, and you don't have friend boys coming around to visit you when I'm not here. I mean, that's not cool."

Never a doormat, Vivian bristled with her own resentments. "You can't come in here after being away all week and start telling me what to do."

"Hold it," I interrupted her. "I'm talking about just plain right. I don't want guys hanging around here any more."

Deep suspicions about the northern ghetto culture poured into my mind at that moment. Since being in Newark and New York, I had observed a different sort of morality from what I had been raised with. I had seen first hand how people could be married, with two, three, four children, and carry on affairs right under the noses of family, friends, and society. If the husband or wife was away a lot, they seemed to be perfectly free to commit adultery with several partners.

If pregnancy occurred, there were always abortions, as many as were needed. Sometimes these abortions were self-induced, and sometimes the women died from them, but they seemed to be an accepted way of life. There were also a lot of illegitimate children in the big cities. There simply seemed to be no deep concern about adultery. Men and women had their physical needs, and they met them. The barriers had long ago come tumbling down.

I certainly was no tower of virtue by that time in my life, having dabbled in most of the worst society had to offer. But because of my background, adultery was abhorrent, particularly on the part of a woman. It was the classic case of the old double standard that existed in society as a whole and in black society as I knew it. Adultery was wrong, but especially was it wrong for "my wife." People sort of shrugged when it came to men, even though it was still serious. "You know how men are," people said wryly. But among women? No sir, there was to be no sleeping around. That produced outrage. Killings resulted. People were shot, knifed, women beaten. *Getting caught* was bad news.

At that moment in Newark, I felt I could be working my backside off up at Stewart, and Vivian might be fooling around with her "friend boys" in dangerous ways, and no one would think twice about it. I was convinced of it at that moment. The tragedy is that it was all very innocent. He was just an acquaintance. But we often accuse people in the areas near to our own guilt. Would it have been just a "friend girl" if the situation had been reversed?

At any rate, I was furious over Vivian's friend, and she got just as angry as I was—indignant, in fact. And the man didn't leave. I did.

As I drove furiously back to the base with my pride and my ego hurting, I conjured up all manner of images in my mind. I was certain beyond a doubt that I had made a terrible mistake in getting married.

I spent most of that night at the bar. If she was going to pull such stunts, then I was going to start hanging out even more. She wasn't going to make a sucker out of me.

Several days later, I was on my way to Saudi Arabia.

9

Awakening

DHAHRAN, SAUDI ARABIA. It sat right on the Persian Gulf, a hotbed of dangerous potential. Many experts thought the world might one day blow apart right in this area. But at that moment in 1962, it was peaceful, and I spent nine fast months that changed my life.

I continued to play basketball and toured all the major civilian oil installations in the area. I moved on with my communications duties, more than holding my own in the Air Force, although the stripes of promotion were slow in coming. I was still an airman third class, and I was getting more worldly all the time.

It is important to remember that, despite the hardships of the previous couple of years—the changes in environment, the insecurities, the questioning—I was a young man very much in love. I loved my wife. I wanted good things for her—for us.

Furthermore, despite the pain of being black in a white society, I loved my country. I was intensely patriotic, for reasons that still elude me. I was an almost ideal serviceman. I thrilled and shivered when the National Anthem was played, I listened carefully when my commanding officers spoke.

But, like all other people, to one degree or another, I was self-centered. An extremely high percentage of my thoughts

during any one minute were about myself. I viewed everything from my perspective. I was at the center of the world.

With such an existential or humanistic viewpoint, I was guar-
anteed frequent unhappiness. First of all, the world is not
made to run that way. God is to occupy the center of existence.
Second, if everyone else was at the center of his world, while
I was at the center of mine, a mighty tug of war was inevitable.
And my happiness would depend upon whether I was winning
or not. It was certain that I would not win consistently.

So I was unhappy a lot, but along with most of mankind,
I figured that's kind of how it is.

That unhappiness exploded into fear and anger one mid-
summer day as I lay on my bed in Saudi Arabia, thousands
of miles from home. I opened a letter from Vivian and read
quickly.

"I am more than three months pregnant," she wrote.

I dropped the letter to my chest and looked straight up.
"There's no way," I said half-aloud. "There's no way you can
be pregnant."

I swung around and put my feet on the floor, sitting upright.
I'm not sure if I spoke aloud or merely formed the words in
my mind. "If you are pregnant, how come you're just getting
around to telling me?" My head pounded. "How come I'm
just now finding out?"

The months crawled by, and the fear and anger deepened.
Suspicion gnawed at my insides. I was certain I had been
betrayed in the most ultimate way by my wife. What was I
to do? I had several more months to go on my tour of duty.
Day after day, the pressure in my chest and belly grew worse.
Thoughts, ugly visions, swirled through my mind.

There was very little to do in Saudi Arabia to relieve the
tension. Because of commitments to the Saudis, the American
bases could not serve liquor to their own people. Messing
with Saudi women posed gruesome threats to one's life at
the hands of Muslim society. So there really wasn't a lot to
do except see the sights, and there weren't any. A really big
night in Saudi Arabia consisted of going with a bunch of your
buddies to the USO club to play bingo and then top it off
with a double milkshake with an egg in it.

We didn't even have a PX at the base. If we needed something, we ordered it by catalog and waited until it arrived at the warehouse.

I spent a lot of time lying in my bunk, staring at the ceiling or trying to concentrate long enough to read a book. I thought too much. Over and over. I wallowed in depression hours upon end.

* * *

In those long hours I was wrestling a lot with the quality of races. As I've noted, I had been taught, usually not so subtly, that people with skin colored other than white were inferior. Over the years I had come to realize that our national leaders, especially southern leaders—senators, congressmen, men of stature—had actually been speaking variations of one theme: "Oh, we love our colored folks, our nigras. We don't hold anything against them. But, you know, they have trouble learning." Then the voice dropped several shades. "They're really inferior, I'm afraid." Then the voice rose a bit. "It's essential that we have these separate-but-equal schools, for their benefit, because they can't keep up with us."

Even when the words weren't spoken this plainly, this was the translation that was heard.

In Saudi Arabia, my thinking was changing. I was seriously questioning this thesis that had been soaked into my character. For one thing, I had found in the Air Force that I could do more than keep up with the whites. I was not burning up the record books with promotions, but I was doing my job well and developing into a reasonably intelligent young man. I wasn't sure I was inferior.

I remember clearly the day this turned into conviction and was pounded into my mind to stay. I was alone, standing out on the flight line, drinking a strawberry milkshake. I was simply watching the airplanes land and take off. Saudi Arabia was a major stop for most of the international airlines, so there was a lot of traffic.

Leaning against the fence, sipping from the cardboard container, I spotted a crew headed toward a monstrous airliner—a Boeing 707, as I remember. There was the pilot and probably the co-pilot, and several other colleagues, and there were the stewardesses. My eye picked up a very attractive one. And they were walking around the aircraft, checking it over, and then they boarded. They were a good-looking crew, smart and crisp.

A few minutes later, the passengers began filing out and the plane gradually filled up. After awhile, the engines fired up, roared a bit and eventually the plane rolled down the taxiway to the runway. It swung out into the middle, charged down the runway with a deafening sound, and lifted into the air. It was absolutely beautiful.

I took a few more sips and suddenly my head snapped up and I watched open-mouthed as the 707 grew smaller with each second. It had dawned on me that the entire crew of that marvelous airplane, fully responsible for that gigantic vehicle carrying hundreds of passengers, was black. The pilot, the co-pilot, the officers, the stewardesses—all would have been classified as colored in America. They were dark-skinned Arabs, with skin like mine, hair like mine (we called them "ragheads"), and presumably brains like mine. And all of those passengers, many whites, had had faith enough in their ability—their lack of inferiority—to trust their lives into their hands.

I stood upright and thought about it. Here I was, in a country of allegedly backward, largely uneducated, relatively poor people—"ignorant, dumb ragheads," in the serviceman's idiom—and a black crew was flying this modern jet airplane without any help from the whites. In the "land of the free and the home of the brave," there were no black pilots, no black crews, and only a handful of black stewardesses.

Following those few minutes on the flight line, my perceptions began to change, first gradually, then faster and faster. First of all, I stopped thinking of the Saudis as "those ignorant, dumb ragheads." I noticed that they were capable of talking to me in English and then turning around and talking to somebody in French or Arabic or something else while I didn't have the foggiest idea what they were talking about. Superior, educated me could only speak English and a smattering of Spanish.

I also was sharply aware of the American oil people working

in Saudi Arabia. Many of them were from the southern United States, and they treated the Saudis even worse than they treated the American blacks.

But it was the removal of the concept of racial inferiority and superiority that most affected me. I wanted to talk to others about blacks as people. I needed to learn, to understand, to grow. I wanted to know what to do with this new awakening. If my intellectual ability was not governed by my skin color, what was I going to do about it?

Also, doubts about my own country started to creep in. Why were so many Americans, who had such marvelous traits in so many areas of life, prejudiced and harsh in their treatment of other races and nationalities? Why did blacks "enjoy" second-class citizenship in the United States? It was the sixties, and my thoughts and emotions were quickly catching up with those of the more radically minded American blacks. I was thoroughly untrained in my philosophy, but for the first time, one was beginning to take shape.

* * *

I needed to do something about my marriage. Thousands of miles from home, I was still burning with confusion about Vivian's pregnancy, about her attitude toward me, and about the benefits of marriage in general, even though I knew deep down that I was very much in love with my wife. I was still terribly insecure, and that made life with me quite volatile.

Discussions with my superiors finally brought word that, since there was talk about possibly closing the base, they would let me return to the States three months early. I arrived in Newark in time for Levi's birth on Christmas Eve, 1961.

That night, instead of going to the hospital, I stayed home and got drunk. Such indefensible conduct can only be attributed to the fear and anger that was gripping me and beginning to twist my life. Although I said nothing to Vivian, I suspected that this new baby was not mine. And that suspicion found good breeding ground in my lifelong insecurity, which fed the fear, which fed the anger, which fed the suspicion.

I sat at home alone, and I drank—until all my tortured imaginings were like scrambled eggs.

The next day I visited Vivian and the baby. Once again,

my heart sank. The boy was light-skinned. Vivian and I are both dark, but I remembered that the "friend boy" from some months past was very light-skinned. Still, I said nothing to Vivian. I'm not sure why I said nothing. I believe fear prevented me. I was afraid of the truth, and I probably was afraid of what both of us might do and say.

With time, I realized I had been wrong. Levi was definitely my child. I had been victimized by the scourge of the universe, fear, which entered when man fell away from God shortly after his creation. Would I ever be free of my own special brand of fear, the insecurity that had plagued me for so long? Can man ever overcome fear and insecurity? I was skeptical.

Despite this, however, my little family eased into the happiest few weeks of its young life right after that. Jealousy, resentment, fear, and insecurity slipped into the background when the Air Force sent me to Langley Air Force Base in Virginia, an area of the world that would hold special meaning for me one day.

We moved into a small apartment and our existence was almost idyllic. We came close together, we snuggled, we laughed, we saw hope for the future—all on about $350 a month, counting allotments and everything. Vivian was a wonder at making our little household work. It was hard to believe that two months earlier I had been near eruption into violent hatred. Little did I know that those seeds were still lying just beneath the surface.

The shattering of the idyl came on Saturday afternoon in downtown Hampton, Virginia. Nigel and I were in a department store, standing in line to pay for the two or three articles I wanted. I remember I was feeding on a large dose of fatherly pride, sharply dressed in my Air Force uniform, holding the hand of the oldest of my two sons, an adequate supply of American dollar bills in my pocket.

Unexpectedly Nigel tugged on my hand. "Daddy." I looked down and smiled. "Daddy," he said softly, "I need to go to the bathroom."

"You'll have to wait just a minute, son." I was a bit nervous because he was in the midst of toilet training and he didn't deserve to go through the embarrassment of wetting his pants since he had done everything he was supposed to. So I smiled at him. "Wait just a minute, pal."

When I got to the counter, I said to the lady waiting to take my money, "Excuse me, ma'am, can you tell me where the restroom is?"

She said matter-of-factly, without any apparent animosity—as if I should have known, "We don't have restrooms for coloreds in this place."

I looked straight ahead for several seconds. My throat became very tight. I was on the verge of vomiting. I wanted to hit somebody—anybody. What was I going to do? For Nigel? For my own dignity? What could I say to the boy? "You'll have to wait? Be quiet? No, you don't have to go to the bathroom?" What could I say to the lady and her superiors? "I'm going to tear this place down? I'll kill you if you don't let my boy use your bathroom?" Whom do you hit? Whom do you punch?

I stared three or four more seconds, and turned around and walked away, dropping the merchandise on the counter. I took Nigel outside, into an alley, and let him wet up against the wall. Hot tears filled my eyes. My mind swirled and raged. "He's no better than a dog," I seethed. "Going against a wall. Why? Because he's cursed with this skin color. Something he could do nothing about." I was almost crying aloud. I pounded my fist into the brick wall. "And this is America—home of the free and the brave."

My little boy looked up at me proudly. He'd done his business like a little man. I wanted to hurt somebody for what I knew they were going to do to my son as he grew older.

I was a twenty-five-year-old black man, and those twenty-five years crashed in upon me. I saw then what I had glossed over most of that time. There was never a day in the life of a black American when he was not in some way humiliated and degraded. Race relations had improved but the indignities continued. As I reflect on these matters from the vantage point of the mid-eighties, grateful for the marvelous changes that have occurred in this truly blessed land and certain that improvements will continue, I wince inwardly over the scars that still remain in black people everywhere. For even in the eighties, prospering as I have as a minister, a broadcasting executive, and a black American, the scars frequently come close to derailing me.

In recent times, I was traveling by car to an executive meeting with a group, all white but me, and several voiced the desire to stop for something to eat. We were in rural Virginia. Before long we came upon a locally owned "family restaurant," and several said, "Let's stop here."

I noticed that there was a national chain across the street, and I blurted out, "Hey, let's try that one. We know it will be good."

But the quality of the food was not my concern. I knew that the chain would accept both blacks and whites. I wasn't sure about the local restaurant in the rural South. And I had dark memories of walking into establishments where you could sense you were not welcome and where fear of a lawsuit was the only reason for serving you. Even when your life has been drastically changed, you seem to carry some scars forever. You are daily reminded that you are different and inferior in the eyes of some.

That incident with Nigel in the department store in Hampton, Virginia, was terribly damaging to me, for I was already on thin ice emotionally and philosophically. As I noted, in Saudi Arabia I had developed a readiness to hear about blacks being people. I was ready to hear what some of the black nationalists were saying. The heat of my instinctive patriotism had cooled.

I was probably a lot like the black GI's who returned from World War II and the Korean War desiring to be treated equally socially if they were to risk their lives equally militarily. I was especially ready to hear that blacks were every bit as intelligent as whites and thus should assume more and more responsibility in society and the marketplace.

Complicating this burgeoning black awareness in me was the immaturity and instability of my married life. True, recent weeks had been good, but even I knew they were not solid. I was in turmoil as a husband and as a black man.

I needed to *do* something. It was obvious that, once again, I needed to get out of the South as quickly as possible. And if I went overseas, I almost certainly would get another stripe, and I desperately needed the money that would bring.

I didn't have to wait long. A roller coaster was on its way.

10

Crime and Infidelity

I LANDED IN TRIPOLI, the ancient Mediterranean port city, one of the two capitals of Libya. The ugliest and the prettiest of twentieth century life co-existed on this historic promontory jutting from North Africa toward the tip of Italy. It was an appropriate setting for a crucial scene of my personal drama, a plunge into deceit and darkness.

For the first three months, I thought of my wife constantly, yearning to be with her. I wrote frequently, and she regularly replied. Then came the monotony, the routine of overseas service. I started hanging out with other airmen to break the boredom, spending a lot of time at bars and private parties. My letter-writing gradually decreased, as did Vivian's.

Bud (pseudonym) was a tech sergeant—short, stocky, and black as the ace of spades. For a number of days, we bumped into one another at parties and seemed to fall into easy conversation every time. He was a smart guy, knew the ropes in the Air Force, and always enjoyed himself. He worked in food service.

Bud and Ben. Before long, we were close friends. Virtually every night we had something going—a party, a bottle, a session at the NCO Club, or maybe just lounging around talking in his room or mine. We enjoyed one another.

At about the same time I was getting acquainted with Bud,

a new civilian secretary, Lois (pseudonym), came to work in my office. Lois was a pretty brunette—white—from Canada. She was just as easy to talk to as Bud, and we immediately fell into light-hearted, fast-talking horseplay, the sort of relaxed friendship I enjoyed with Bud. She was a good sport.

One afternoon, in the midst of kidding around and laughing about Canadians and Americans being stuck in the far-off desert world, I asked her if she'd like to go to a movie. She paused for a split-second, and looked right into my face. "No," she said slowly. "I think not."

"Why?" I shot back. "Prejudiced?"

"Of course not!" she recoiled.

"Then why won't you go to a lousy movie with me?"

"Has it occurred to you that I simply might not be in the mood for a movie?" She was trying to keep her cool, but I knew I had her on the defensive.

"I'll bet!" I scoffed. "You've surprised me. You're prejudiced. A bigot. A racist."

She began to blush under my onslaught and I knew I had her. I turned and walked out, but I'd be back. I had plans for her. I bided my time a couple of days and then I asked her to go to the NCO Club with me. She hesitated again, but the previous encounter was still fresh in her mind. She wasn't a racist, but how to disprove the charge? Finally she surrendered. "Okay. I'll go."

I had used a technique on Lois that was fairly new at the time, and still widely used today, I might add, by both blacks and whites. On the political front, public figures must avoid the racist tag at all cost. To coerce these leaders into supporting even obviously ridiculous social programs, black leaders sometimes threaten to accuse them of racism. Often the media picks it up, and there are few political leaders who will dare to risk the flak of being called a racist. The tactic will almost certainly be felt sooner or later by anyone who dares to stand up against any ill-conceived social engineering program. It is applied impartially to blacks as well. If, for example, a black should oppose busing, or racial quotas, then he is also branded a racist. Black conservatives find themselves charged with "reverse racism"!

So poor Lois didn't have a chance. Our relationship had started out light and airy and fun. But it soon turned heavy. One false step leads to another. The Bible says it clearly: ". . . man is tempted when he is drawn away by his own lust and enticed. Then when lust hath conceived, it bringeth forth sin; and sin, when it is finished, bringeth forth death."[1] It didn't take long.

"I think I'm pregnant," she said to me one evening.

I was twenty-six years old, married, the father of two children, raised in a Christian family, knowing right from wrong. And I looked her right in the eye. "Get rid of it."

She looked down for several seconds and then back up. "How?" she asked.

I was on a roller coaster by then. "I'll see what I can do."

The next day I talked to a friend in the dispensary and he gave me some pills. "This ought to do it, Kinch," he said.

The pills did not cause her to abort, but they killed what I thought of as a fetus, and she had to go to a black market physician downtown for a regular abortion. The next day she talked sadly about it.

"You know what, Ben?" she said softly. "I saw it. They took it, and it was a baby. I saw it."

I responded, "Well, that's tough." And the calluses closed around my heart. "When are you going to be back in action?"

A man's heart can become very hard. This woman was telling me she had seen a dead baby—my baby—and I didn't care. I wanted my pleasure, the feeding of my own ego, and I wanted it as quickly as possible. Vivian and Nigel and Levi were a long way from that moment. Lawlessness, the kind I would one day find described on the pages of the Bible, had settled in. I would ultimately be responsible for the murder of four unborn babies. It was a long, long way back to Uvalde, Texas.

* * *

The partying intensified. A good time was all that mattered. Drinking, eating, sex, hanging out, doing as little work as possible were the primary points of concentration. But we—Bud and I—needed money for our escapades. The pathway was becoming more demanding, and slippery.

I found that Bud really did know the ropes. We were able to move very softly but swiftly into the black market, selling American cigarettes and all manner of goods from the commissary and PX. Bud was perfectly positioned for stealing the products we needed, and I showed a talent for hustling from servicemen the coupons that were required to purchase cigarettes and booze. We bought them at PX prices and sold them in downtown Tripoli for a nice profit.

Crime was easy, I found, and it financed a decent lifestyle if you played it cool and didn't get extravagant.

One extravagance does stand out in my memory, however. It grew out of an idea for a big party, the granddaddy of all our big parties. "We have a villa," Bud said as we laid our plans. It would accommodate dozens for all manner of activities. What a bash we would have. We even got a kick out of planning it.

"Hey, man." Bud came up with a brilliant idea. "Let's get a hog!"

"What?"

"A hog!—you know, let's roast a whole pig."

"Great!" I laughed. "We'll do the whole bit."

And we did. We dug a big pit and roasted this huge pig all day long until it was just perfect. People came from everywhere—those we knew in the Air Force, people we'd met in our black market dealings, nightclub people. A black African prince showed up, along with several high-born African ladies. And several showgirls from a Tripoli club added considerable charm and sex appeal. Liquor flowed freely, and it was a swinging time.

One of the most unsettling moments in my life up to that point occurred as the party was going full blast. People were standing all over the place; some were lounging on sofas and easy chairs. A general hubbub prevailed. I was walking around from group to group, thoroughly engulfed in the festivities, and I turned a corner in an alcove to find myself looking into a big, full-length mirror. I slowed and stopped, and for a few seconds—it seemed like a minute—I stared and didn't recognize the reflection in the mirror. Time really stood still. I was keenly aware of everything. But I didn't recognize the man in the mirror—because he was black. I realized that, for that short period in my life, I had not thought of myself as black. I had forgotten I was a Negro. Skin color had vanished from my perceptions. I had been immersed in an environment in which black was merely a biological distinction, not a cultural one. No one mentioned skin color; no one mentioned racial inferiority. "I've got blue eyes; he's got blond hair; you've got dark skin." That's the way they thought. The American perception of a difference was gone.

It was a stunning revelation to me. And something happened. Something changed in me that moment; something that began back in Saudi Arabia was completed. I, a black man, was as good as anyone else. The exhilaration of that moment was unbelievable. I was launched like a projectile held back by a rubber band. I was loose; I was soaring; I was free-wheeling.

I laughed out loud and stared back into the mirror. There I was—tall, slim, hair beginning to show some gray even at the age of twenty-six, mustachioed to overcome a baby face, and smart. Cool, baby.

That surge of awareness was costly in some ways, however. I intended to hang out from then on in places just like that with people just like that; I intended to live it up. And that required money. And that required more lawlessness. I did more black marketeering, everything imaginable. I became so lawless and so rebellious against authority—always discreetly, however, always underground—that I took on a nickname: Pagan. It was apt. I was a pagan, through and through, especially considering my upbringing. I stayed cool on the surface, but I was devious, deceptive, quick to seize any opportunity to feed my own appetites. After all, I was as good as anyone else, and I deserved life on a platter—right that moment.

Flooded with the exhilaration of my new awareness, I spotted a blonde German girl, a dancer, in a show at a Tripoli casino one night. Bud was with me, and we took her and another woman out after the show. *Now, you have arrived, baby.* I didn't speak the words, but they permeated my thoughts. *You have arrived, Kinchlow.* The Canadian girl had been good. But she was a brunette. This girl was a blonde—tall, statuesque, the epitome of the white man's freedom. I had a car, money in my pocket, and a blonde by my side. Pagan was worshiping at the world's altar.

Another time, I picked up my new blonde and took her to the NCO club at the base, proud as a peacock, aware of the appreciative, envious eyes of the blacks upon me and my date, but also of the hate-filled glances from many of the whites. It was sometime after five o'clock, and we entered the base at the front gate, driving right to the club for a quiet, leisurely dinner with all the trimmings, drinks, wine, everything. I did most of the talking at first, telling her about the United States, Texas, Uvalde, and about the places I had been in the Air Force. She grew increasingly comfortable and told me a lot about herself. It was an auspicious beginning, and I was basking in it. I see with hindsight that I had in a way taken leave of my senses; I was in a kind of insanity. I had forgotten who I was, what I was. I was completely unaware of being black. I was having the time of my life with another human being.

The evening moved along, and at one point, I toasted life with good cheap NCO Club booze. The dance music started up. It was not bad, and the setting was adequate. I had toasted more than was smart or I would never have done what I did next. I asked her to dance.

We moved easily around the floor, nice and slow and romantic at first. Then the music swung into a fast number and we started to boogie. Suddenly, wham, someone bumped into me. It was a hard blow in my upper back. Well, those things happen when you're jamming. We kept dancing. Wham. There it was again. I looked around and there was this good-sized, rugged airman—white—dancing with a woman—white. I was stunned by the look on his face. It was contorted, red, fierce. He was in a rage.

Then he swung his partner around and obviously tried to hit me again. I side-stepped the blow.

Instantly, the past poured in on me. It all came back. The bubble burst. I was not like everyone else. I was different. I was Black Sambo, out dancing with Snow White. I was black, and there was more to this thing than having blue eyes or blonde hair. It was more than biological. It was a mind set. Rage poured over me and turned my mind into a swollen mass.

I started to move toward the other airman, but the German girl tugged on my hand. "Please," she whispered, her face terrified. "Please don't cause a scene." She tried to pull me toward the edge of the floor. "I'll get in trouble. They'll pull my passport and work permit, and I won't be able to work, and I'll be in trouble. They'll send me back to Germany."

We went back to the table, paid the check and left. I knew something was going to have to give. I had traveled half way around the world. People had accepted me. I was welcome everywhere—but home.

* * *

I drove slowly out of the base, exiting through the back gate and heading toward the Mediterranean. We didn't talk a lot, a few words about how crazy the world was and how people really didn't like people, especially those different from themselves. Gradually the tension from the club slackened and we enjoyed the magnificent view. At one point, we stopped on a promontory and got out of the car. We watched a ship way off in the distance and could occasionally detect the low, drawn-out sound of its horn. I remember being swept up in the moment and murmuring phrases about "ships passing in the night" and "ships lost at sea." It was pretty dramatic, but it seemed to fit my mood. I felt lost, adrift.

I took her to her hotel and then drove back to the base, returning through the back gate. As I approached my barracks, I saw several squad cars and a number of military policemen buzzing around. Parking, I had a flash of concern about whether they were on to my various black-market schemes.

"Naw, they're not swift enough for that." I spoke the words under my breath. "Besides, it would be the CID boys, not the military police."

I went on in and went to bed. Nobody paid any attention to me.

I had been asleep a couple of hours—it was about two o'clock—when someone came into my room and shined a light in my face. It was a buddy of mine, and I heard him say, "Well, here's Pagan. He's in bed."

That's all he said, and then he flipped the light off and left. I was too drowsy to give it any more thought.

The next morning, quite early, a call came through to my office. "Kinchlow, report to Air Police headquarters."

Something was up. Maybe they had found something after all. The old fear roared through my entire body. *I'm going to jail,* I thought. *What can I tell them? I've got to think of something. Should I run? Where would I go?*

I walked into the police headquarters, my mind churning, racing. An officer looked up. "You Kinchlow?"

"Yes."

"What did you do with that white woman?" His face was tight and hard.

"What do you mean?" I asked. My mind went blank. I wasn't sure what was going on. This wasn't what I expected.

"You know what I mean. You came on the base yesterday afternoon at five o'clock with a white woman, and you didn't take her back off the base. Where is she?"

I simply stared at him. Hundreds of people had come onto the base yesterday, why they were so interested in me?

The officer rode right over my silence. "What happened to that woman? We saw you bringing her in at the front gate. Where did you take her?"

He looked down at his desk for a moment, then back up into my face. "Kinchlow, did you sleep with that woman?"

So this was the heart of the matter. His principal concern was whether I, a black man, had gone too far with a white woman. I knew there would have been no concern whatever if I had been white, or she had been black. Whatever lingering doubts I may have had about the white man vanished. Here was the fear openly expressed: "Let them in our schools and businesses and they'll be in our beds."

I started to say, "No, I didn't sleep with her," but I merely looked him in the face. Several seconds of silence passed. Finally, he said, "Okay, Kinchlow, you can go on back to your squadron."

They hadn't caught me doing anything, so there was nothing

they could do about their suspicions, but my squadron made
sure I had a nasty job for several weeks—trash detail—cleaning
the washrooms, picking up cigarette butts, and so forth.

* * *

Inside, however, my tailspin into hostility—fear and anger—
was nearing completion. Rage, rage against America and
Americans, had built to a climax in my recent experiences
with awareness, blackness, unblackness, and then blackness
again. I was no longer merely smoldering; I was raging. I
was a capped inferno. Here I was, a soldier who had sworn
to defend his country and its constitution, a young man sent
overseas theoretically to help defend the freedom of North
Africans, whom the swaggering Americans looked down upon.
Yet the only time I felt human was when I was in the society
of non-Americans. Americans immediately made me feel sub-
human.

Riots against Americans erupted in Libya about that time
and they produced a kind of perverse satisfaction in me. The
American forces were issuing every type of warning against
leaving the base and especially against going into downtown
Tripoli. One young white medic, disregarding the warnings,
was found after his car had been stoned and turned upside
down. He had been raped and stabbed to death, with something like seventy wounds left in his body.

However, blacks apparently could move around in total
safety, and did so. Those who lived downtown continued to
live there and the rest of us frequented the night spots as
we always had done. The Africans never bothered us; indeed,
they seemed to like us. They saw us as oppressed people,
just as they saw themselves. Without talking a lot about it,
we black Americans saw things much the same way. There
is an unmistakable camaraderie between many oppressed colored peoples of the world.

My thoughts began to jell. I could see that I was not part
of a minority, but of a great majority: the colored people of
the world. The white people were the actual minority. "Yankee, go home" didn't faze me now. They weren't talking to
me, brother. I was one of them. We together were going to
overthrow the racist dictators, our mutual oppressors.

I spent a lot of time in a Tripoli bowling alley during this time, but did very little bowling. I had discovered a pocket of Communists—the Marxist influence was very heavy in that part of the world, especially in Rabat, Morocco—who hung out late at night in the bowling alley. One fellow was especially fascinating—small, scrawny, pock-marked, a typical archvillain. He wore a patch over one eye and chain-smoked for hours on end. I was amazed that his fingers were stained brown all the way up to the hand, from constantly holding a cigarette.

Night after night we sat and talked. We drank a lot of wine and smoked, snuffing our cigarettes out in bottle caps that we used for ashtrays.

"We'll beat you," he said, meaning the West in general and the United States in particular. "We'll beat you, and you won't even know it until it's too late."

"How, man?" I asked through the haze. "There's no way you can beat us. We've got the best military machine in the. . . ."

"Sure you have," he interrupted. "You've got the army and the planes and the money, but we've got something else."

"What's that?"

"We believe in what we're doing. We believe it." He stared steadily at me with his one, muddy brown eye. "We believe it. You don't believe in what you're doing. We'll beat you."

I had to admit—if only to myself—that he was probably right about belief, especially if I was any example. I didn't believe in much of anything, certainly not in my country the way I had just a few years earlier. I wasn't sure where my beliefs were headed, or even what they really were anymore. All I knew was I didn't believe what I had once believed— the kind of things I had learned from my scout leader back in Uvalde.

As a result of those bowling alley talks and an unfolding realization of the numbers of nonwhites in the world, I had started to read about Marxism with enthusiasm. I also began to dabble in other philosophies of unrest, like the black muslims and other black nationalists. This certain guy Malcolm X was making a lot of sense, it seemed from afar.

One thing was certain. I had no use for religion. It definitely was the opiate of the people and was to be flushed out of society. It was for weak people, not those who wanted to make radical changes.

I can remember expounding in the bowling alley in the late night. "Religion is something the white man gives us to keep us busy while he slugs us and breaks one jaw, and we turn the other cheek and he breaks the other jaw. As Malcolm X says, 'It's like novocaine that the dentist puts in your jaw while he breaks it.' You're sitting there feeling no pain while you're bleeding to death. If you get enough religion, you feel no pain. I don't want nothing to do with it."

Everything I had learned from my mother in those early years and from my dad later on washed right out of my consciousness. If there was a God—and I wasn't sure there was—I wanted nothing to do with Him. He was obviously white.

* * *

What about my responsibilities back in the United States while all this was taking place in me? It might seem contradictory in view of my crazy, free-wheeling conduct—my crime and infidelity—but I still loved my wife. I was concerned about her and my two boys, although I wrote very infrequently. To my consternation, Vivian did the same, writing less and less until the letters virtually stopped.

She did tell me, however, that she had taken an apartment of her own in Newark and that the children were with my parents in Texas. I wondered about this at times when I was not totally engrossed in my own pursuits. *Living by herself in New Jersey . . . in an apartment by herself. . . . The kids aren't even there. . . . And I'm not hearing from her any more. . . . What's going on?* But even as I spent more time and money on me, I sent little besides an allotment home. Vivian was virtually on her own.

I had no idea what was going to happen in my life. How would my new attitude play back in the States? What would Vivian think? She was black. She had to understand how I felt and thought.

11

Kill

TO MY SURPRISE, THE AIR FORCE sent me home from Tripoli a month early, bound unhappily for Shaw Air Force Base in South Carolina. Why couldn't I keep out of the South?

A stopover in Newark revealed part of the reason for the decline in Vivian's correspondence. Not only did she have an apartment, but she also had a boy friend. It was no "friend boy" this time. It was a boy friend—married, but still available enough to spend plenty of time in Vivian's apartment.

I confronted Vivian, and she readily acknowledged the truth of the report. "That's right," she said matter-of-factly.

* * *

I was assigned to a tactical mobile outfit at Shaw, which meant I was on the road a lot for all kinds of training exercises and alerts. When I was alone, I did a lot of thinking. Somehow I had to deal with my situation; I had to settle things with Vivian. One day a plan emerged.

On Friday afternoon I flew into New Jersey unannounced. Late in the day, determining that no one was at home, I sneaked into Vivian's apartment. I was carrying a bottle of whiskey and a butcher knife.

I started to work right away on the whiskey and reviewed my task. It was simple. The entrance opened into the kitchen; I would sit there quietly and let them have it when they entered. Both of them. I would go for him first. The only requirement was that I move quickly and surely.

I continued sipping at the whiskey. The hours passed. The whiskey was gone. And I passed out on the floor.

Adding to my sickness the next morning was the fact that Vivian had not come home, alone or otherwise. I was desperately sick, and my rage no longer boiled within me. It lay heavy, like death, in my stomach—quiet, sullen, stinking.

I returned to Shaw.

* * *

Two weekends later I was back in Newark, determined to succeed. I went into the kitchen, unscrewed the overhead lightbulb to guarantee darkness when Vivian would reach for the switch. I stood in the middle of the room and pondered my position. I would stand behind the door, just outside the room. As they entered in the darkness and Vivian flipped the switch, she'd head for the living room to turn on a light and he would follow her. While they were crossing the dark kitchen, I would make my move. I would kill him with the butcher knife. Then I would kill her. We'd have to see what would happen after that.

I sat in the dark for about an hour. It seemed much longer, but I sat patiently, waiting, sober, no liquor this time. The knife lay on the floor. This was it.

I heard someone coming up the stairs. It had to be them. I picked up the knife, stood up, and poised myself.

I heard the kitchen door open and then a second later the flip of the light switch. Nothing happened. Then, right on cue, Vivian said, "Something's wrong with this light."

With that, I stepped out, ready to stab. But I was early. Vivian recognized me immediately and apparently saw the knife, or at least an object in my hand. She screamed and slammed the door between her friend and me. I was left standing in the darkened kitchen with my wife.

Darkness, confusion, chaos. That summed up my life in that instant.

Vivian paced the floor, striding two or three steps and then swinging back for two or three steps, turning abruptly, back and forth, almost in a straight line. Both of us were shaken by what had almost happened.

I leaned against the wall, not knowing where to look or what to do. I was exhausted, and my chest pounded. The rage was there, but inactive.

Many minutes passed, in virtual silence, except for our heavy breathing. Finally I began to try to talk.

"All I want is for you to come with me . . . down to South Carolina . . . so we can be together . . . and try to work things out," I mumbled, barely audibly. "We've got to work things out."

The dark silence continued. In the street below, there was the sound of a horn, and a screeching tire, and a yell. "Okay." All was silent. "Okay," she said with great heaviness, "I'll come down there." Later on, Vivian told me something I had not known about the man who had "gotten away" in that incident in Newark.

"You know, Ben," she said, "he always carried a gun. If you had opened the door, he would have killed you."

* * *

We began to work out arrangements to get the children back from my parents in Texas and to find a place to live in Shaw. As these plans were being worked out, however, I began to hang out and mess around with other women, none of it especially "serious"—just wrong, dead wrong.

Politically, I had been merely drifting for several months. My own personal problems had overtaken my concerns about the future of blacks, the nation, and the world. I was too self-centered to spend a lot of time worrying about others. I wanted my own happiness, and we were trying hard to work it out. Still, neither Vivian nor I, even with the children back, was truly satisfied. We were going through the motions of trying to develop a life. I was still smoldering and simmering down underneath. And the racial prejudice that was so deeply rooted in South Carolina didn't help any. The practicalities of everyday life—finding a home to live in, shopping, eating in black-only restaurants, riding public transportation—kept rubbing the wounds raw.

Then my Air Force outfit was ordered to the Dominican Republic to support the Marines who were sent in to try to stabilize the ongoing turmoil against the current regime. Castro was in place, and Latin America was seething. My earlier unrest was ready for advancement and crystallization. I was ripe for radicalizing.

"Yankee, go home!" That's what did it. I ran headlong into the hostility of the local citizens. It had not been like that in northern Africa, where the natives thought I was on their side because I was black. This time they saw the uniform and yelled, "Go home!" Inside I yelled back, "Hey, I'm one of you!" But, no, I was an American, a Yankee imperialist, and I was hated at home and abroad.

This triggered further confusion. Back in South Carolina, I was hated because I was black, not "American." There in the Caribbean I was hated because I was an American. I didn't belong anywhere. What was wrong with me? Could I find a place anywhere?

I was there only ninety days, but that was long enough for me to seize upon black nationalism in a serious way. We blacks were going to have to fight back. The white man was the target. The white man—we made it sound like a swear word—was the enemy. The system would have to change. It would have to be brought down.

As I'd discovered superficially in Africa, Malcolm X and his cohorts were worth listening to; they had answers.

By the time I got back to South Carolina, I was a bundle of lightly controlled anger and determination. I began to talk to anyone who would listen about the evils of the white system. My knowledge of the growing black nationalist movement increased. I became keenly aware of the depth and breadth of discontent throughout America. I saw that revolt was just beneath the surface. And I was glad.

* * *

Vivian and I continued to try to make some sense of our domestic life. She wasn't much interested in my radical she-nanigans, so I continued on that road without her. But we were together, and that was something.

Quite abruptly, however, even that was overturned; I received orders to go to Okinawa. It would get me out of the South, but I might be heading for another "Yankee, go home!" situation. It was an accompanied tour, which meant I could take my family. But it also meant I'd have to reenlist, and I wasn't sure I wanted to do that, given my anti-American state of mind. So before committing to taking my family and reenlisting for four more years, I said I'd go alone and check out housing and other living conditions.

But could my fragile family situation handle such a separation? Was I making another terrible mistake? What would I find in Okinawa?

12

Hatred

WHITE AMERICANS SIMPLY DID NOT understand what black Americans were feeling in the twentieth century. In some peculiar way, they believed that through the years, even the centuries, the blacks had basically been content and happy just the way they were pictured—singing, dancing, picking cotton. "The Negro people are a happy people," they thought. They had failed to detect the resentment simmering inside black people generally against second-class citizenship, against being forced into certain roles, against being labeled as inferior.

Black Americans were masters at dissembling in front of whites. They never said—to whites—what they truly thought. The white man, perhaps earnestly, would ask the black man, "How is everything, Joe?"

Joe would grin and glance from the side or to the ground, and say, "Everything is just fine. Everything is lovely."

And the white man would think, "Our colored folks just love us. They're such a cheerful, happy people. Isn't this a wonderful land?"

A paternalistic attitude, a sentimental, mushy deception, was inevitable. And with it naturally flowed a white conviction that said, "We aren't doing anything wrong."

Consequently the average white American never realized the depth of resentment and bitterness that was building. And the so-called "black leaders"—promoted to their positions by whites—were no help. Indeed, they did a disservice to the blacks by assuring "the Man" that all was well. This was the way they kept their jobs, and if trouble started to brew, it was the black leaders' job to get it straightened out. "Everything is okay," they told the white establishment. "It's lovely, yes sir. We're in favor of separate but equal treatment. Yes sir. It's okay." There were some who spoke the truth, but they didn't stay around long.

Obviously fear underlay all the deception. Yet deep anger grew within the fear. As we've noted, fear surely is the scourge of the universe, taking root within the creation at the time of the Fall. And it is certain to produce anger, for fear cannot lie alone in a person forever. It must eventually produce an action against the feared object. Man, for example, feared God after his first disobedience to Him in the Garden of Eden. He tried to hide himself but couldn't. The fear ultimately produced action against God—rebellion against Him, rejection of His authority, and finally, attempts to remove Him from public life, as so many nations have done in modern times.

But most white Americans missed this buildup of black resentment, and the eruptions of the sixties caught them totally by surprise. Many whites looked at one another and asked, "What's happened? Why are these nice colored people suddenly so upset?"

The same sort of thing has happened to America in connection with other countries around the world, especially the lesser developed countries populated by "colored peoples." The countries wanted the American dollar and American technology, so they hid their resentment against what they perceived as a paternalistic attitude on the part of the United States. They did not speak truthfully when asked, "How is everything?" They gave the same kind of answers the blacks had to whites, "Oh, everything is fine."

Suddenly, entire nations were shouting, "Yankee, go home!" and "We hate you, America!" The United States was stunned.

What had happened so suddenly? Actually, nothing had happened suddenly. It had been building for years, just as it had
previously for Great Britain and France. If there was a difference in America's situation, it lay in the fact that blacks for
years believed that someday America would acknowledge
their loyalty and give them the kind of citizenship the Constitution promised.

Their patience ran out in the sixties. Blacks took to the
streets, cities burned, blood flowed. "What's wrong with you?"
the whites screamed. "What is it you want?" Many, many
whites honestly did not know.

* * *

The years of the racial turbulence have been carefully docu-
mented, along with the changes and progress—and lack of
it—that they have produced. But for the purposes of clarifying
my pilgrimage, it is important to understand the significance
of an unusual man named Malcolm X. In my assessment, he
represented the deep yearnings that had been suppressed
for years in the hearts of millions of blacks, including the
so-called black bourgeoisie that lived and worked within middle America. Most of us were frustrated and angry, but lacked
the proper articulation. Malcolm *said* what we *felt.*

"The white man's society is totally corrupt," he said. "It
has no redeeming value." Malcolm argued that history made
clear that wherever the white man went, he subjugated those
there ahead of him. Missionaries would arrive first and the
natives would accept them. Then would come the men with
the guns and they would rape and pillage and colonize. He
pointed to continent after continent and event after event—
the Boxer Rebellion in China, the colonization of India, the
enslavement of Africa. The white man forced China open
to the opium trade, fostered the addiction of thousands, and
brought in guns when anyone complained. No matter where
he went, Malcolm declared, the white man oppressed those
who were weaker, made treaties (and broke them at will)
with the stronger, and converted the rest.

Malcolm pointed to the American Revolution to illustrate
white hypocrisy. The new world colonists rebelled against tax-

ation without representation, while at the same time enslaving blacks kidnapped in Africa. The great early-American leaders like Washington and Jefferson had slaves at home to do the menial tasks, he said, while they sat down to hammer out a Constitution that declared all men created equal and with certain inalienable rights. This militant black nationalist preached that racism was ingrained in American society. I—and millions of other black Americans—agreed with him.

Malcolm drew on one of history's most ringing declarations from a famous early American leader, Patrick Henry, for his solution to the black man's plight: "Is life so dear or peace so sweet as to be purchased at the price of chains and slavery? Forbid it, almighty God. I know not what course others may take, but as for me, give me liberty or give me death!"[1]

Patrick Henry was a great patriot, Malcolm said, and blacks were merely saying the same thing Henry had said, but they were not called patriots, but traitors, radicals, and dangerous revolutionaries. Malcolm assured us we were not radicals and un-American. To the contrary, we were the true patriots. He stirred the hearts of many black people across America with those words.

Malcolm's strategy differed from that of another famous civil rights leader, Martin Luther King. The latter urged blacks to demonstrate in the streets but carried nonviolence to the point of offering themselves as sacrifices to the likes of Bull Connors in Birmingham, who resisted demonstrators with violence. That did not appeal to me.

Malcolm urged people to go into the streets if necessary in defense of their rights, not touching anyone, not promoting violence in any overt way. However, he said, if anyone touches you—in defense of your person, your liberty, your family—"send him to the cemetery." He advocated the practice of the same kind of violence or nonviolence that was practiced by the opposition. If the opposition fought, then the blacks were encouraged to release every bit of retaliatory force they possessed.

There was no way, Malcolm emphasized, that the black man was going to reason his way effectively with "this totally corrupt individual," the white man. The black American would have to get his civil rights the same way the white

American got his—through armed, violent revolution in the face of armed, violent opposition. Black separation would be required.

Many whites at the time did not recognize Malcolm's great appeal to the broad black community. They thought he was an extremist, when in fact he represented the thoughts and emotions of a huge number. He was a charismatic leader— well spoken, thoroughly articulate, reasonable sounding, and attractive.

For many years Malcolm devoted himself to Elijah Muhammad, the titular leader of the Black Muslims, who argued that the white man was the literal incarnation of the devil. Malcolm spoke at huge Muslim rallies and also participated in well-publicized forums at Harvard and other institutions, in televised debates, and in radio talk shows. Despite many grave doctrinal errors, the Muslims preached a strict moral lifestyle that helped their followers. Stay away from drugs, they said. Eat a proper diet. Dress decently and modestly. Avoid alcohol and nicotine. Stop sexual promiscuity. Save your money. Start your own business. Respect your elders.

Malcolm, who was thoroughly loyal to Elijah Muhammad, was shattered when the latter, living in a big mansion in Chicago, was discovered to have had affairs with three of his secretaries, leaving all three pregnant. Malcolm appealed to Elijah to repent and apologize publicly, but the leader refused and resorted to cover-up. Malcolm was forced out of the Muslim movement, but his massive emotional following continued until his philosophical goals began to shift gradually toward good will and equality and less hatred after he made hajj, or pilgrimage to Mecca.

In a day that rocked black America in the mid-sixties, Malcolm was gunned down, with evidence pointing toward a group of Black Muslims presumably acting in retaliation for Malcolm's charges and separation from Elijah Muhammad. I was convinced that the blacks had lost the one man who, if he had chosen such a role, could have united and led black America into armed revolution.

* * *

Even after his assassination, I continued to be greatly affected by Malcolm and his writings. I felt that many of the other traditional civil rights leaders were wishy-washy, egotistical pawns of the white establishment, not men determined to lead blacks into full liberty in this country.

Throughout these months and earlier years of radicalization, I grew in intensity of commitment to black nationalism and crystallization of my own ideas to promote black freedom. Such talk more and more dominated my conversations. I would sit for hours with friends or mere acquaintances—in bars, at parties, in the barracks—debating the course of the country and the sense of discontent, oppression, and anger that was obviously rising within blacks everywhere. I spouted so much of Malcolm's philosophy, with my own special twists, that people started calling me Malcolm Z.

I had learned from the military that it is unwise to engage in confrontation until all the pieces are ready to fall into place. Thus I nurtured plans for a boycott of the PX's over the lack of black business products and for organization of the black community into action groups, but in practical terms I did little more than talk, seeking to build enthusiasm and support for future action. One obstacle was that black military men were understandably fearful of damaging their careers. They had worked a long time, and despite being angry and resentful and willing to talk about it over drinks at the NCO Club, they were unwilling to put their stripes and allotments on the line.

Possessing a vivid imagination, I was more impulsive and more readily able to see the possibilities of success, so the reluctance of others upset me. That, coupled with the fact that I had less rank and less to lose, led me to more inflammatory ideas and remarks, and my reputation as a radical spread. In fact, word went out that Kinchlow was becoming a troublemaker. They were to keep an eye on me.

My basic goal was to unite blacks against what I perceived to be the racist society and government of the United States. I knew we had to get organized, but I was lacking in details of how I would organize. I probably fell short of actually wanting to bring the Government down—which many wanted to do, of course—but I wanted black power, a black voice in the direction of everything. If whites were not going to give blacks equality, then blacks should seize it. I wasn't sure what that actually meant. With hindsight, I recognize that if the reins of power had been handed over to me, as I seemed to crave, I wouldn't have known what to do. I had no real idea of how to run a government, national, state, or local, or even of how to run a department. But I knew there had to be change. Blacks had to rise up. The fear and resentment and anger could stay down no longer. They had been suppressed, choked back, for decades and generations, despite the blindness of most whites. An eruption was certain.

In Okinawa while I planned and waited for the revolt I felt was sure to come, I decided to pick up a deadly—but legal—concealed weapon. Karate. That was the answer. I needed to learn karate. I needed it for my own personal problems and it would be handy for my longer-range, black nationalist goals. The martial arts would be important. Especially those that can maim and kill so swiftly and silently.

A friend pointed me in the direction of an Okinawan master, a Sensei of the Okinawan style, which was more deadly than the Japanese, I was told. And, truthfully, my purpose for studying karate was to learn to kill—to kill brutally and painfully.

I was single-minded. I worked hard. I'd leave my job and go to the dojo and work until I was ready to collapse. I slept, ate, did my job, and practiced karate. That was my life. I was being driven by hatred.

Hatred is a terrible motivating force. It doesn't stand still, but spreads out into everything you touch, throughout your mind, your body, your relationships. I was ruled by hatred. The Malcolm X philosophy, the black nationalism, the rage against America—they all blended in with my anger at my wife and my burning fury over her lover. All the inferiorities of my childhood, all the slights from my youth, all the racial insults toward me and my children, all the ugliness of drinking and carousing, all the evils of adultery and abortion poured in upon my inflamed brain. And all of that was being mixed with my karate studies in roaring intensity. Revolution was churning.

I began to fill writing tablets with ideas and schemes for the future. Plans were slowly taking shape. I immediately was struck by the financial need if blacks were to move ahead, so I drafted thoughts about a black bank. If ten million black Americans each made a one-time deposit of $10, this bank would be capitalized with $100 million, virtually overnight. It would be a start, I wrote, and would help get the white man's foot off the black man's neck. We would no longer be so totally dependent upon the whites for our mortgages, loans, and credit card financing. If a "brother" ran into trouble over a civil rights stand, the black bank would carry him. The bank would grow rapidly as it reaped appropriate interest off transactions with blacks all over America.

From there, black business would blossom everywhere. Before we knew it, the blacks of America would have the third or fourth largest economy in the world. It sounded good on paper.

I didn't stop with finance. My karate lessons kept my mind channeled toward the use of force, particularly in a military manner, and my tablets bulged with thoughts of violence.

I figured that a smart move would be to round up the young black gangs that were already so violent and vicious on the streets of the cities and discipline them in karate and other guerrilla warfare tactics. Discipline would be the key, as I was learning in my lessons. Then they could be sent back, not as gangs, but as disciplined bands—troops—to cover New York, Detroit, Chicago, Newark, Los Angeles, and the like. They would be a united force, not wasting energy and their necks with independent little bursts of violence, but set to move in vengeance if the whites sent their police forces against any black demand for rights.

At the same time, my notes said, we could teach self-defense and ranger tactics to hostile young blacks in Mississippi, Alabama, Georgia, Florida, Louisiana, turning them loose into the countryside like guerrillas. We could arm them with M-16's and if trouble developed with the likes of Bull Connors we could send a crack hit-and-run troop in, clean up, and then disappear into the countryside again in the manner of the Southeast Asian and Latin American revolutionaries. The blacks in the countryside would support and take care of them, grateful to have someone fighting in their behalf.

While the militaristic activities were proceeding, political force would be applied by people like Martin Luther King, whom I actually considered to be an Uncle Tom but perhaps useful along with the N.A.A.C.P. to put unsettling and unnerving pressure on the judicial and governmental system. Linked with the violence and threat of violence, this force would reshape the crumbling system into one more pleasing to blacks.

Driven by hatred, I made my plans.

* * *

The racial future of America was at stake.

The future of my marriage and family was at stake.

My personal future—my life—was at stake.

What was going to happen? My country hated me—I hated me. My own morality was a mess, but that never occurred to me. I had been wronged, I was the wounded one. Somebody had to pay.

Thoughts of revenge, anger, and hatred seemed to be my only foundation. They infected everything. I was on a collision course with mayhem.

13

Break-up

JUSTIFICATION. It comes from the word "justify," essentially meaning to declare or make right. The Scriptures say we are justified—declared right or made right with God through faith. This is a powerful concept in God's Word. It gives us right standing with God, apart from works. It is grace, God's free, unmerited favor, by faith in Jesus Christ. It's the why, the raison d'etre of our standing, our ability to come before God; it's the root of boldness in prayer, for expecting miracles.

Justification is also a reason for murder. Cold-blooded murder.

Before a person commits an act of any significance, there must exist in that person's mind the justification for the act. As long as one can justify the deed, declare or make it right, the deed can be done. Adultery, for example, must be justified in the mind of the adulterer: "My wife doesn't appreciate me". . . "My husband doesn't romance me". . . "We're in love." Abortion must be justified: "I'm too young". . . "My career". . . "Too many children already." Divorce, strikes, arguments all result from an attempt to justify our position. This kind of justification does not need to be rooted in truth or in fact. No one else needs to see or grasp the "truth." All that is required is that the perpetrator of the act be able to justify a particular course of action in his own universe. "This is true," I say, so it follows that whatever course I adopt is justified.

When, after returning on emergency leave from Okinawa to Sumter, South Carolina, I decided I'd kill myself, grabbed a handful of sleeping pills the Air Force had previously given me and gulped them down, my action at that moment seemed to be justified. "I was provoked—driven to it." It didn't take long to realize the stupidity of that move, however. I was killing the wrong person. So I yelled for Vivian. She rushed into the room, and I told her what I'd done.

"Whatever happens," I said, "don't let me go to sleep. Keep me walking; keep me moving. If I go to sleep, I'll die."

I made myself vomit, and then for several hours Vivian walked me back and forth across the room and forced me to drink strong black coffee. Eventually I shook off the effects enough to survive, but for two days I was in a fog.

Later, when I decided to "off" my enemy—"waste him," commit cold-blooded murder—in my mind there was suffi-cient provocation. "My pain, my suffering, my anguish" my suspicions and my jealousy were proper justification. It doesn't really matter what the "cause celebre" is, the reasons for mur-der are as many and varied as the types of murders committed. Ask any who have killed in deed or in thought—"the murder is justifiable."

I remember the day well. I took Vivian to the commissary and bought about a hundred dollars worth of groceries. We took them home and stacked them in the kitchen. Then I went downtown and bought a .25-caliber automatic and shells. From there I drove to the base and parked by one of the dining halls. I stood around for a minute and then stopped two men.

"Hey," I said, "I'm a friend of O. C. Smith's and I just got in from overseas. I'd like to see him. Can you tell me where he lives?"

I think there was a possibility they might have known who I was, but they didn't say so. One pointed toward a barracks down the street. "Sure, he lives in that barracks right over there," he said.

Touching the cold metal of the gun in my pocket, I got

back into my car and drove down the block. It was going to
be murder in cold blood.

I went into the building and stepped into a foyer. The CQ—
the man in charge of quarters—sat behind a table over to
the right. He looked up.

"Can you tell me where Smith's room is? O. C. Smith?" I
asked.

It turned out that Smith, as we saw in the prologue, was
away on temporary duty. Someone had thwarted my plans.
Someone had other ideas.

* * *

With my two boys huddling in the car, crying and confused,
I drove away from the house in Sumter, leaving Vivian crying
on the front porch. We had nothing but the clothes we wore—
no fresh underwear, no toothbrush, no nothing. I drove
straight through to my parents' house in Uvalde.

Mama met me at the door, weeping softly, her face etched
with grief. In the days that followed, the fatigue and the worry
settled into deepening lines. I hated hurting Mama, but I was
still angry, still determined, and in no mood to be tender
and forgiving.

I went immediately to see a lawyer, Taylor Nichols, and
told him I wanted a divorce—then. I spilled out everything
about Vivian, with names and details. Taylor listened, saying
little. I was very much the aggrieved party, offering very little
information about my own escapades.

"I don't want a reconciliation," I blurted. "I want a divorce,
and I want it now." I was getting angrier by the minute. "I
don't want any argument. All I want is my kids."

Taylor made notes and looked at me. I wasn't at all sure
he intended to do it the way I wanted it done.

"Now, I have to go back overseas," I continued. "Here's
your deposit." I pushed a wad of bills toward him. "Can I
get a divorce while I'm overseas?"

Taylor, with much the expression of a lonely hound dog,
looked down at his desk, then at me. "Yes. We can have the
papers sent to you." He paused. "When will you be back?"

"In two months."

With that, I returned to Okinawa, leaving the boys with my parents in Uvalde. Vivian was alone in South Carolina.

* * *

"She's dying." That was the next word I heard. Mama notified me that Vivian had arrived in Uvalde, within a few weeks after I left, to stay with my parents and a siege of hemorrhaging had landed her in the hospital. She deteriorated quickly.

"You ought to take emergency leave," Mama wrote. "She's really sick."

"Tough," I replied. "I'm not coming back now."

And with that I threw myself deeper into my black liberation work, making myself extremely unpopular with Air Force authorities and some of my fellow airmen. Of course, a sizeable number of the black servicemen agreed with me, but few were as aggressive as I. In fact, I was getting more and more radical, actively pursuing efforts to boycott the PX's and organize blacks into action groups.

One day in early 1968 my superiors called me in and said they were going to send me to Korea, where tension with the Communist forces was heightening as matters worsened to the south in Vietnam.

"I'm not going to Korea," I said flatly. "I'm not going to fight your imperialistic white man's war. I won't go."

The Air Force reply simply was, "You are going or you will be discharged." My enlistment would run out the following July, and if I refused to go to Korea I would be mustered out then.

"Then I'll get discharged," I replied. I needed only seven more years to complete my twenty for retirement, but I said, "I'm not going."

In July, 1968, I left the Air Force—the fellow who had intended to remain in the service forever, the fellow who used to get goosebumps hearing "The Star Spangled Banner."

I—Malcolm Z—would pursue my revolutionary goals in the States. Who knew what would happen to the rest of my life? Who knew what would happen to Vivian? To Nigel? To Levi? Who cared?

14

Getting Ready

EVEN THOUGH VIVIAN WAS NOW living at my parents'
house while she got over her illness, I decided to head home
for Uvalde and go to school. My kids were there, and my
parents, and my brother, Harvey. It was a place in which to
get a toehold on civilian life and decide what to do next.

As far as Vivian was concerned, I figured I had Taylor Nichols hard at work on my divorce and I'd be able to get her
out of my sight and my life soon.

I rarely said a civil word to her, but she had decided at
this point that she wanted to try to make a go of our marriage.
I had the goods on her and as far as I was concerned she
was an unfit mother, so she was afraid of losing the boys.
She was still weak, but genuinely wanted to try to make some
kind of stable life for us all. Of course, Mom and Dad were
in complete agreement with her, and the kids could hardly
wait to get us all back together in our own place.

For the whole family, living with me was like living in a
mine field—you never knew when I was going to explode—
and I lived in my parents' house as if I owned it. For instance,
their insurance man, an old white fellow, had been coming
around regularly for years to collect his premium. Instead
of knocking on the door, he'd stick his head inside and yell,
"Hello? Jewel?" calling Mama by her first name. If she didn't
show up immediately, he'd walk right in.

I observed the process once after I got home from the service, and the next time he stuck his head in the door, I bolted out of my chair and stopped him about two steps into the room. I towered over him by at least a foot, murder in my eyes. Using my forefinger like a steel rod, I jabbed at him with every word.

"Don't you *ever* walk into my mother's house again without knocking," I grated through clenched teeth. "I mean, not *ever!*"

I loved the surprised, scared look on his face, and I hung around glaring at him while Mama fumbled to get his money to him and get him out the door before something else happened. She was humiliated and embarrassed by my rudeness.

Instead of apologizing to my folks, I yelled, "It should have been done years ago!" and burned with contempt for my Dad's kind of Christianity that tolerated such patronizing from Whitey.

"That's not happening to *me!*" I stormed. "I mean, there's not gonna *be* any of that garbage! The white man is telling us to look yonder to heaven to the land of milk and honey while he's got his right here and now, and I'm not turning the other cheek and waiting for heaven."

Nostrils flaring, eyes like slits, I finished the lecture. "I want mine *now!*"

Mama wiped the corner of her eyes with her apron, sighed as though she had the weight of the world on her shoulders, and retired to the kitchen for peace and quiet.

I'm sure my folks must have wondered at times where God was. My younger brother, Harvey, was way out in front of me in his revolutionary thinking. My philosophy was, "Let's go out and negotiate with the white man for our rights, and if they don't give them to us, let's blow 'em up." Harvey's was, "Let's blow 'em up first and negotiate with the survivors."

In between my tirades, the atmosphere in the house was like a tomb. It seemed like the divorce proceedings were taking a long time, but I soon got so busy I didn't take time to check it out.

* * *

I decided for certain at that point that I didn't intend to further the black revolution by risking my neck in the streets with Martin Luther King tactics. Malcolm X was dead, and I didn't plan to join him. Neither was I going to be one of those poor, ragged revolutionaries with no place to go. I was going to be a revolutionary, all right, but from inside the system.

I knew that the leaders who fight the wars sit behind the big mahogany desks and make the decisions to send the troops out into the streets. After listening to all the rhetoric of the people who were running things, I knew I was as smart, if not smarter, than they were. So I made up my mind to go to school—get an education. I intended to major in business with emphasis on sales because that was where the big money was. That would give me the power and influence I craved.

I also had determined a long time ago where the power and control lay in the black community. I needed to be a preacher. Preachers and school teachers had more influence in the black community than anybody. My plans had nothing to do with any religious feelings, because, as I noted, I had gleaned from my Marxist reading that religion was the "opiate of the masses," a poor escape for the oppressed. No, it was simple. With words and with a pulpit, I could stir the people toward revolution. Besides, as a preacher, I'd be supported by the black church and wouldn't be dependent on the white establishment for bread.

With these "lofty" goals in mind, I enrolled as a freshman at Southwest Texas Junior College in Uvalde in the Fall of 1968. Even though I was a self-styled revolutionary and a third-degree black belt and a veteran, I was more than a little nervous throughout the first semester. In spite of everything, I found I still carried the residue of the lifelong inference that blacks were inferior—and the reason we needed separate but equal schools was that we couldn't keep up. So when I came as one of three blacks to this junior college of 1100 whites, I came with quite a bit of inner turmoil, half expecting to fall, but buoyed by my Air Force experiences and angry enough to risk it. I made up my mind that if they beat me, it wasn't going to be without a struggle. And if I failed? Weren't blacks supposed to fail?

The first day in class seemed to confirm my worst fears.

These kids—some looked young enough to be my own—lolled back in their seats with their feet on their desks, chewed tobacco, threw spit balls, flew paper airplanes, and in general seemed to be bored. I tried desperately to take notes and hear and remember what the teacher was saying. And though I was working part time, I put in every spare minute studying. Indeed that whole first six weeks I worried about how much harder I was working to learn than the white students were. Maybe they were right—whites were smarter. Here I was busting my hump and these kids didn't even have to pay attention.

Finally the day came when the first grades of the semester were to be posted. I figured I might as well face the music, and went straight to the D roster looking for mine. I couldn't find my name and I thought, *I didn't even get a D! I failed!*

With a pounding going on in my chest and my mouth dry, I made myself walk over to the failing list. No Kinchlow. I took my first deep breath since coming into the building and dared to look under the C's. It wasn't there either.

I swore bitterly. *Those guys didn't even put me on the board!* There it was again. Discrimination! Then I thought, *Well, I'm here. I might as well look at the B's.* I wasn't on the B list, either. I assumed there wasn't any sense even looking at the A list, but it might be interesting to see who the top students were. And that's where I found it. "Kinchlow, Ben," right there in alphabetical order, in every subject I'd taken.

When I saw that, I knew if I could make straight A's carrying the schedule I was carrying, then I obviously wasn't inferior. In fact, I reasoned, I was superior. If there had been any doubt left in my mind that the wrong people were running things, the good grades erased it. From there, I moved on like gangbusters. I was free to soar. I piled up a string of A's, a couple of B's from "prejudiced teachers" (actually men who bent over backwards to help me in math courses) and when I made my first talk in speech class, the rest of the students applauded.

I became a regular on the dean's list and a national junior college scholastic society elected me into membership. The students then elected me president of my class, and before long, I faced a run-off for the presidency of the scholastic society, but since I was already president of my class, I thanked them and let the other guy have the honor. (That was better than going through a run-off—made me look big in declining and erased the possibility of a defeat.) Eventually I was listed in *Who's Who in Small Colleges in the United States.*

Even though I was married, albeit separated, had a family, and held a job, I jumped into campus life and made a name for myself, even writing a column for the college newspaper. It was sometimes a shade crude—and revolutionary. But it was well received. I was having a taste of recognition and success, and loving it.

During a talent show I did a stand-up comedy routine, smoking a cigarette and telling jokes, one pretty off-color. I stole the show. Most of the jokes also happened to be stolen—from vintage black comedians.

This reception and success didn't change my feelings for whites. It just convinced me that I had always been used and manipulated, but nobody on campus suspected how I really felt except the blacks and perhaps one or two teachers.

* * *

Even though I thrived on the attention I was getting, I faced a grinding daily schedule. Vivian was working by now as a teacher's aide at Robb Elementary and involved in direct sales part time. I found the perfect job for me, and it fit neatly into my schedule of classes.

I became a test driver with the General Tire Company, driving cars to test the quality and durability of the tires the company manufactured. Every weekday, I drove a 444-mile run on an eight-and-a-half mile oval track on the outskirts of Uvalde, working from 4:30 in the afternoon until 1 in the morning. Then I'd get up the next morning in time to be in economics class by 7, and finish my last class at 2 in the afternoon.

When the college asked if I'd like to teach a class in self-defense, the only free hour of the entire day that I could muster was from 2:30 to 3:30 in the afternoon. I said okay. I didn't stand to earn any money from teaching the class; it was strictly a volunteer deal. The payoff came in other ways.

As an instructor of a martial arts class, I participated in a little ritual that was worth more than money. At the beginning of every class, the students had to get on their knees, face forward, and on a signal from the assistant in command, bow to the instructor.

Picture this: a black, six-foot-five, 215-pound, third-degree black belt karate instructor dressed in a black gi, standing arms akimbo in front of rows of bowing whites. I ate it up. Things seemed to be moving along right on schedule.

Then, new tragedy struck. The very peaceable Martin Luther King took a bullet in his brain while enjoying the evening air from a hotel balcony. It didn't seem to matter to white America how the black people chose to fight—with Malcolm X's tactics or with Martin Luther King's—the whites won either way.

With the deaths of Malcolm and King, I was left with a gut full of hatred and rage and an increasing desire to vent it in destroying the system that had put it there. I had spent years getting ready for a giant revenge party that had been postponed, as far as I could see. Yet I knew I—and indeed all blacks—had to push on somehow.

For me, college still seemed to be the key. I had thrown away almost everything else. I had run out of things that I'd considered worth getting up for in the morning. They'd disappeared one by one. I had tossed out the moral standards my parents had believed in because I had found them impossible to keep. Where I had once been patriotic to the core, the very thought of my country now made me sick to my stomach. Marriage? A trap, a farce, nothing but heartache.

Now what do I do?

I think I must have subconsciously decided to keep moving so fast I wouldn't have time to think, and to use booze to anesthetize what couldn't be ignored. With my job and the GI bill and what Vivian was making, we had plenty of money and a good car. The Mexican border lay just sixty miles to the south, so a couple of nights a week after getting off work at one in the morning, I'd floor board it over to Piedras Negras and drink and party a couple of hours. This put me in great shape for my seven o'clock class the next day. I felt like I was holding on to a live wire most of the time—if I had a chance to sit down I couldn't stay put.

* * *

One day a few months before graduation, I showed up for the karate class wondering how much longer I was going to be able to keep going, when in came this little sawed-off guy with sandy hair and a brown belt in judo. A light bulb turned on in my head. He wasn't much to look at, but maybe he could give me a hand with the class. After the session I called him over.

"Hey, man," I said as I looked down at the top of his head; he couldn't have been more than five and a half feet tall. "You a student here?" He smiled and brushed his sandy-colored hair out of his eyes. I noticed he had a long nose.

"My wife is," he answered, his voice quiet and easy on the ears. "School of Nursing. I also have a daughter in school here."

Without hesitating he offered me his hand, which was about half the size of my own. "My name's John Corcoran."

"Pleased to meet you, John," I said, anxious to get to my point. "Say, I notice you're a brown belt. Do you think you'd be interested in giving me a hand during class?"

I could tell by his expression that he was glad I'd asked him. "That'd be great," he said in that same quiet voice. "I'd like to do that; I sure would."

"All *right!*" I said. "Next week too soon?"

"Be fine," he said and turned to pick up his stuff. "See you then."

I watched him walk away. *He ain't much,* I thought, *but he'll have to do.*

15

Corcoran

CORCORAN SURPRISED ME. He was good at martial arts, and after the first class, I knew he was going to be a big help to me.

Even though he was good at teaching self-defense, he seemed perfectly at ease in the world—comfortable and friendly with people. It bothered me that such an insignificant appearing little guy could be so at ease with himself. But it also roused my curiosity.

One day after class we fell into conversation about karate and, noting that I had a little extra time before work, I asked him if he'd like to get something to drink in the Student Canteen.

"Sure. Let me stop off at my car and leave this stuff," he said easily, motioning toward his gear.

We stepped outside into the sunshine and he trotted a few feet away to his car—a Nash.

It figures, I thought. *He drives a Nash. Nobody drives a Nash.*

I swung in beside him and we strode across the campus to the canteen, making small talk. We ordered tall glasses of orange juice and I started my investigation.

"Well, uh, John, uh, what do you do for a living?"

"Actually, Ben, I'm a minister. I have a ministry to students here on campus."

Whoa boy! I thought, trying not to laugh. *I got me a live one!* I had learned a long time ago that certain things irritate people, having made it a practice in recent years to be quite an irritant. At that time in history, if you wanted to agitate the average white guy, you bad-mouthed America. But if you wanted to rile a preacher, all you had to do was bad-mouth the Christian faith and the church.

"Well, well, well," I laughed. "So you're a preacher. What church?"

He seemed as undisturbed as before and finished a long drink of his juice. "Christian Missionary Alliance." He said it as though I'd recognize it right away.

I thought, *I never heard of it. Can't be one of the big ones. That figures, too.*

"Good thing you're not Baptist," I drawled. " 'Cause the Methodists don't like the Baptists, and the Baptists don't like the Episcopalians, and the Catholics think they're all nuts. Makes you wonder if there's anything to any of 'em." He shook his head, slowly and sadly. "That kind of thing makes the whole world wonder, Ben," he said softly.

I didn't seem to be getting anywhere with this guy. "I understand that right here in Uvalde on a Sunday morning, you can hear the Baptist church on the corner singing, 'Will There Be Any Stars in My Crown?' and the Methodist church across the street singing, 'No, Not One! No, Not One!' "

He spewed orange juice down his front and I thought I had him, but when he got his breath, he burst out laughing! Nothing was working; I couldn't upset him. I could feel the frustration building up inside me. I decided to hit him with my favorite observation about Christians.

"At least among the Buddhists and the Moslems and the Communists, they agree on what they're after. The Chinese Communists and the Russian Communists agree that America has to go even if they disagree on how. The different kinds of Muslims may disagree on the strictness of their religion or how they should practice it, but at least they all agree there's one God and his name is Allah." I glared at him for a second. "In the Christian church, they don't agree on anything!"

John leaned back in his chair and seemed more comfortable than ever—as though he were ready to spend the rest of the day there.

"I think you may be mistaken about all the harmony in the Communist party and among the Muslims," he smiled sadly, "but you are a hundred percent right about the Christian church."

The tension fizzled out of me like air out of a punctured tire. Instead, I found myself wondering how much he knew about Marxism, and Islam. Before I knew it, we were knee deep in the philosophy of religion.

The thing I couldn't resist about Corcoran was that he listened to me. In our conversation that day I never doubted that he was interested in what I thought, whether he agreed or not, and that he believed I had a right to my opinions. He let me spout off and wind down, and when we parted company that day, I felt a little less raw and uncomfortable with life.

The after-class trips to the canteen became a ritual, and even though I spent many of them ranting and raving about racism and discrimination, I couldn't resist going. I knew there were times when I embarrassed John with my tirades and occasional explosions, but he was always ready to go back with me the next day.

"Don't tell me about the American way," I'd rave. "It's liberty and justice, all right—for Whitey!"

John would look at me with sad eyes—the same kind of expression Taylor Nichols had had in his eyes the day I had ranted and raved in his office about how bad Vivian was and how I didn't want to talk reconciliation. It was as though they knew something crucial about me but couldn't find a way to tell me.

After a while, I recognized something else in John's eyes. He genuinely liked me and I knew by then that he was no wimp. He was wholesome and solid and good. This was a guy who had somehow figured out how to handle life and not let it tear him apart, but I guessed it was because he was white. Life was easier for him.

We talked about everything under the sun, and eventually

we talked about Vivian and the mess our marriage was in. One day when his wife drove up in the Nash to get him at the canteen, he introduced me to her. Her name was Joy and I could tell he thought she was somebody special.

I thought, *I can't believe this! She's like every preacher's wife I've ever seen!* She was what you'd expect a missionary type to be—eyeglasses and prematurely gray hair—but nonetheless quite attractive. When she said "God," it came out "Gawd." Yes, she was nice, but she was more overtly Christian than John, so I was immediately suspicious.

As I said, John was not overtly religious. He never preached at me. If I wanted to talk about politics, we talked about politics. If I wanted to talk about religions, we talked about religions. But then one day, when he'd missed lunch and ordered a cheeseburger, he glanced at me casually before he started to eat.

"Mind if I pray?" he asked offhandedly.

"I ain't no heathen," I shot back. "Go ahead and pray."

I expected him to do it the way everyone else I'd encountered did, something like: "Dear Heavenly Father, thank You for this food that You have provided from Your bounty, and we ask Your blessing upon it. Amen." That's Texas—Bible Belt—and nobody thinks it's strange if you pray like that before you eat. Just don't overdo it, that's all.

But right there in the canteen, this guy starts to *talk* to God. I mean he *talked* to Him, just as though He were there. It caught me off guard. If I'd had a hat on, I would have taken it off.

I was so surprised, I really don't remember exactly what John said, but it was just friendly talk, just plain bread. He started right off, "Father"—no flattery, no buildup, just "Father," as though He really were his father. Then he said something like, "Father, I really do appreciate this cheeseburger, and I'm awfully glad to be here with Ben, and to talk about all the things we like to talk about, and to get to know You and one another better. I thank You so much. In Christ's name. Amen."

He probably said some other things, too, but it wasn't forced or exaggerated. It was real. I'd never heard anyone talk to God like that. It took the wind out of my sails, and I ate my potato chips in silence.

* * *

A few days later, John brought me a message. "Joy says she'd like to have you and your family come over for supper Saturday night. How about it?"

"Well, that's mighty nice of her," I replied, pleased at the invitation. "I'll check with Mom and Dad and see if they can get loose."

"Joy says she'd really like for you to bring Vivian," John said, and I had the feeling that he would like it, too. It didn't sound like such a good idea to me, but by the time we split that day, I had promised to ask her to come.

I put the invitation to my folks and Vivian at the same time. Mom and Dad were tickled to death to have me ask Vivian to go anywhere at all. I'm sure they said yes right away to make sure Vivian would say yes.

On Saturday night Joy Corcoran had outdone herself preparing the meal. The table sparkled with pretty dishes and silverware, colored napkins and flowers—everything. Dinner smelled good, and turned out to be great—chicken breasts, no less. We chit-chatted for awhile as we ate, and then because I almost never thought about anything else, I turned the subject to racial discrimination.

My dad wiped his mouth and tried to lighten the subject. "I do think progress is being made," he said gently. "Given time, I think we're going to see some changes made. I don't believe the whites really understand how unjust the system has been."

Rage started like scalding oil poured over and through the top of my head. It felt as though my scalp was coming off. Part of me whispered, "You can't do this. You can't blow right here. Not now."

But I went out of control. I couldn't stop. I poured out hate and frustration in front of everyone, virtually ruining a beautiful dinner party. I was vicious in my tongue-lashing of white society in general and John Corcoran in particular, whom I set up for that moment as the surrogate of everything that needed to be changed.

But instead of yelling back at me, John sat quietly, listening to every word, occasionally nodding his head in agreement, now and then lowering his eyes to his plate. But for most of the time he stared into my face.

Eventually, as I noted earlier, the tears spilled from his eyes and streaked down his cheeks. He was crying—not because he was embarrassed or angry with me, but because he cared. He cared for me, the angry, overwhelmed, black, young American.

In that instant, I knew somewhere inside that he loved me with a love that exceeded anything I had ever felt for anyone or anything. That man *loved* me.

* * *

John Corcoran was apparently the first person I'd met whose genuine concern for me as a man had been felt by me. I had had people say they liked me, but I had always believed there was an angle to their affection. I had sensed a selfish concern. I know I had been that way myself.

But even though I couldn't define it clearly that Saturday night in Uvalde, I encountered at that dinner the sort of concern and compassion Jesus spoke about so much and that His followers later wrote about in the New Testament. I know now that John was living out Paul the apostle's appeal to the Christians that they "bear one another's burdens, and so fulfill the law of Christ."[1] Although I was not yet a Christian, he actually had taken upon himself my suffering and frustration, thoroughly identifying with me. He fully recognized that I had a lot of things wrong in my life and attitude—I was off the wall in many ways—but he fully recognized the reality of my struggle. He also fully perceived my desperate need for Jesus Christ and for deliverance from that awful burden.

Those realities caused him to weep for me, in much the way that Jesus cried out over the blindness, pain, and hardheartedness of the leaders of His people: "O Jerusalem, Jerusalem, thou that killest the prophets, and stonest them which are sent unto thee, how often would I have gathered thy children together, even as a hen gathereth her chickens under her wings, and ye would not!"[2]

Yes, I was not able to articulate the details that Saturday night, but I knew somehow that I wanted what John Corcoran had. Somehow, I also knew that I was going to die if I did not find something.

16

High-Speed Turn-Around

"I CAN'T FIGURE OUT WHAT'S wrong with you," I said to John Corcoran a few days later. "You got me. Nothing seems to get under your skin. You think your wife's the catch of the century. You seem to get a kick out of what you do for a living. You don't even seem to mind driving that crummy Nash!"

I wondered if he could tell how serious I really was, how much I hoped he would tell me his formula.

John chuckled and seemed to be looking for the right words. He concentrated on the styrofoam cup in front of him, tearing tiny pieces off the rim. Finally he leaned back in his chair and stuck his hands in his pockets and took a deep breath.

"I'm going to give it to you straight, Ben. I have a personal relationship with Jesus Christ."

"Aw, man!" I groaned, screwing up my face as though I had taken a bite out of a lemon. "Give me a break!" That wasn't what I wanted to hear.

"Sorry, pal. You've heard it before. There's no other way but Jesus. He's the answer. You're finally learning what the questions are. And we've all got 'em. I know what you're thinking and feeling because I've been there."

"Huh," I grunted sarcastically.

"I wasn't always a preacher, Ben," he went on undisturbed. "I used to be a butcher in Chicago and I know what the hard, workaday world is. I used to run the streets a lot in those days. I eventually got down and out—booze and all the things that go with it. I wound up in a storefront mission, and eventually accepted that I couldn't handle my life. I asked Jesus to take over. It was just that simple. I know He's there, and that He's calling the shots. He's God, He loves me, and He knows what He's doing. There's a lot of peace of mind in that."

Everything in me rebelled. John was a preacher. I wanted what John *had*, not what he *was*. *Not religion, man. Don't give me religion!* I was thinking. *Tell me you've been studying under some master for fourteen years. Tell me you sit cross-legged on a flat rock in the desert, or the secret's in eating brown rice, or macro-biology—anything! But don't give me religion!*

* * *

Out at the track, I spent the rest of the daylight hours as I drove thinking of all the dead, churchy people I knew, and of every bored hour I'd spent inside churches. I thought of the time I'd joined the Catholic church in San Antonio, really intending to make my religion work. I had tried to live a clean life, and I knew I couldn't do it. Obviously, John Corcoran was a better man than I was. Too much water had run under the bridge at this late date. Getting religion would mean trying to patch things up with Vivian and I wasn't about to stake my life on that.

I lit a cigarette and realized I was smoking nearly two and a half packs a day. My lungs had started making a funny little sound way down deep. I wadded the pack and threw it hard against the floorboard. Outside the window I noticed the dark settling around me, and I thought, *Here's one more day of my life over with. I wish it didn't have to get dark.*

I recalled a lecture from the foreman when I'd first gone to work at General Tire. "If you ever see a disabled vehicle out there on the road at night, be sure to stop and pick up the driver. This is rattlesnake country. It's uncommon, but people have seen rabid coyotes out there, too."

I switched on the radio—KTSA out of San Antonio. Hard rock—Top Forty.

I took a deep drag on my cigarette and started to sing along with the tune. My mind wandered to what I would do that night after I got off work. Mexico, some booze, a woman—then back in time for school in the morning. Suddenly I realized I wasn't singing the same tune the radio was playing.

I was softly singing an old Negro spiritual. I shook my head. *Hey, this is crazy!* I thought, and turned up the volume on the radio. I picked up where I'd left off with the pop tune. I concentrated and determined not to let my mind drift but a few seconds later realized I was singing the same song again.

"What the—!" I swore out loud, but in less than two minutes I was back at it. I was singing, "My heavenly Father watches over me."

This time I left the volume knob alone as scene after scene from my past flashed through my mind . . . .

The day I borrowed a friend's car to deliver black-market goods and chose to go out a different barracks gate, not knowing the Air Force Police were waiting for me along my usual route. "My Father watches over me."

The day in South Carolina when I stood outside a door with my hand gripping a revolver, ready to blow away someone who, as it turned out, just happened to be away on temporary duty. "My Father watches over me."

The time in South Carolina when my friend rolled his car and died while I sailed through the windshield and skidded to a stop on soft grass. "My Father watches over me."

Had He been watching over me? I felt as though something way out of the ordinary was going on, that maybe He was close—closer than I had ever dreamed God would come to a human being. Could He be close enough to hear what I said? I started talking.

"Okay, God, if You're really out there—I mean, if You are *really* there—and if Jesus Christ really is the Son of God—if You can do anything with my life, please change it. But *don't* give me any religion! If that's all You've got, You can keep it."

And instantly I knew—I mean, I *knew* God is real. Jesus is the Son of God! And at the exact same time, a terrible sense of shame or sin overcame me. I had always had a filthy imagination. I never looked at a woman without sizing her up in lust. I'd dabbled in homosexuality, incest, bestiality. I'd lied in situations where the truth would have served me better just because lying was so easy for me. I felt my soul had been sliced open by a straight razor, laid bare, and there was no place to hide.

All I could think to say was "I'm sorry!" I wept. Great, heavy sobs echoed off the roof of the car. I couldn't catch my breath. "I'm *sorry*, Father!" I had never cried like that before. The huge, shuddering sobs wracked my being, coming from way down somewhere inside me from a place that nobody had ever touched before—nobody!

Even the hatred and bitterness caused by prejudice, or my wife, or the hurts of childhood—none of it had ever touched me down inside where this thing had reached. Something broke loose there and the sobs, floods of tears, poured uncontrollably.

I couldn't stop crying, but I knew I had to. If I pulled off to the side of the road, one of the other drivers would be stopping to check on me, and no one ever saw me cry—no one. I realized I couldn't keep driving much longer because I was getting low on gas. Somehow I had to pull myself together and go into the break room to face the other guys while I had my car gassed up. I could see how it would be; I'd go into this dingy little room with the whites and the Mexicans—greasers and pepper bellies—sitting and staring at my red, swollen eyes. How was I going to pull that one off?

I had to do it, so I found a handkerchief and wiped my eyes and blew my nose. Taking a couple of deep breaths I strolled sheepishly into the fly-speck of a room. The guys hardly noticed me, but I noticed an incredible change in them. They weren't greasers and "pecker woods"—they were just people. Some were overweight, and some were scared, and others were angry, and some were prejudiced, and some couldn't care less about anything. They were just plain, ordinary people. It was the first time since before I could remember that I'd looked at a group of people without dividing them into categories—black or white.

I grabbed two sodas and headed back outside in the dark

toward the track. I wanted to figure out what was going on.
The night seemed friendly, and I felt as comfortable and easy
as if I had been in my bed at home. No thoughts of a loup-
garou . . . I looked up at the sky, and I knew God was there,
somewhere beyond the brightness of the moon.

I wanted to talk to Him, but I didn't know how. I tried to
remember how John had talked to Him, like he was just having
a little conversation with Him. I lit a cigarette, and that
seemed to make it a little easier, so for the rest of the shift,
I smoked and talked to God and smoked and talked. He was
too polite to mention my smoking, I guess—more so than
some Christians I met later on. He just listened and loved
me.

Usually by the end of my shift, I was dead beat and could
hardly stay alert enough to get home. I got in after three in
the morning, having been up since six the morning before.
I was wide awake and excited. It seemed a waste of time to
go to bed and to sleep—not to be conscious of a whole new
world that had settled around me like a warm blanket on a
cold night. I thought of John and how he would understand,
and how glad he would be. I could see us laughing about
my "getting religion," and the last thing I remember is smiling
to myself as I drifted off to the deepest, best sleep I'd had
since I was a kid.

*   *   *

When the alarm went off two hours later at six o'clock, I
came wide awake, feeling like a kid with a new toy, but on
a giant scale. It was *all* new—a whole new ball game. I now
knew what John Corcoran knew—that God loved me, that
He was in control of my life, and that He knew what He
was doing with it.

I went to school feeling almost hyper. Something fantastic
had happened to me. And all those white boys out there were
not white boys anymore; they were just young, dumb kids
who didn't know their elbow from a hole in the ground.

As soon as I could find John, I took him over to the canteen
and told him what had happened to me.

"That's *great!*" He half jumped out of his seat. "Ben, I can't
tell you how happy I am!" He paused, looking for a moment

into my face, thoroughly serious. Then he smiled, "It's really happened. You rascal! You son of a gun! I *knew* it would happen!"

After that we spent even more time across the table from one another, always running out of time before we ran out of things to talk about. So I began to spend time with him on week-end evenings, walking and talking.

Shortly after that I began to feel it was wrong to be apart from my wife and kids. I knew that Vivian was ready to get back together, so on a Saturday afternoon I dropped by to see her. We talked for a few minutes and I got around to the point.

"Have you thought any more about me coming back home?" I couldn't read what she was thinking, but there was a lot of feeling in her voice when she answered me.

"Yes, I've thought a lot about it. The boys miss you. They're getting to be more than I can handle without a man in the house. Besides, it costs a lot to keep two houses going. We could have so much more on two salaries. It makes sense."

She looked tired. I thought of how much we had both changed. Her hair was black—she hadn't dyed it in years—and she had put on some weight. My hair had started graying when I was less than twenty-five years old, so there wasn't much black left in it. She had turned out to be a good mother, a steady worker at the school.

Everything has changed, I thought. *We ought to talk about it.*

At the same time, I knew Vivian was not big on talking; she was a private person. I'd spent a lifetime running off at the mouth, and I knew she was tired of it. I had the feeling that it might be better not to hash over the things that had caused our problems to begin with. That was the past, and I suspected talking would just bring back the old animosities lying just below the surface.

I knew that all I had done to her was covered up in what had happened to Jesus at Calvary, and I certainly didn't have any right to ask her for any apologies. So I just smiled at her and nodded.

"Yeah," I said. "It's high time I came home."

I didn't feel any overwhelming passion for Vivian at the time, but I did feel a new liberation in my marriage—a chance to start all over again from scratch and make it work. I didn't have to tell her what had happened to me; she picked it up right away because I was so much easier to live with—at least for awhile.

My folks were absolutely delighted to hear I'd been saved. My mother had been praying for me for nearly thirty-four years by then. She had prayed my dad into the kingdom, and now I had come in. The three of us were hoping my brother, Harvey, would be next. He was living in Houston and still trying to whip the world into shape by force. The last episode we had heard about occurred when a fellow drove up behind Harvey on a packed freeway in Houston. When Harvey didn't move out fast enough to suit the guy, the fellow honked. Junior (we always called Harvey "Junior") piled out of his truck and landed with both feet on the guy's hood. He jumped up and down three or four times, proceeded to kick a dent in the guy's door, climbed back in his own truck and took off. Obviously, Mom had her prayer work cut out for her.

* * *

As for son Ben, he now felt ready to really straighten the world out. It's a little embarrassing to look back at those days. I mean, I just knew what had happened to me needed to happen to *everybody,* especially those dead, churchy people with all the religion. I figured all that was necessary was to have me tell them about it. After I'd been saved all of ninety days, I felt I knew all the theological secrets hidden for centuries from other mortals.

Dad was so convinced God had called me to preach that he let me have his pulpit at the Methodist church now and then and much to my surprise, once the novelty wore off, the same "sleepers" slept right through my sermons just like they did my dad's. Can you believe it? So I turned up the volume and it helped for a while.

I started studying the Bible in earnest, because these people needed straightening out. I had seen an ad for a *Thompson Chain Reference Bible,* a red-letter edition that I really wanted, but the price was out of sight—$49.95. I thought,

Lord, I'd sure like to have a Bible like that, but I couldn't see spending $49.95 for a Bible. I figured I'd have to make do with my old *King James.*

Even studying that, I thought I saw right away the cause of a lot of people's problems. For example, if it wasn't for the way women dolled themselves up and wore all those miniskirts, I concluded, we guys wouldn't have the problems we had with lust. The next Sunday morning I preached at the Baptist church and when I stepped into the pulpit, I found myself looking straight at a pair of young lady's knees—and more. Even though she couldn't have been more than twelve years old, I didn't hesitate.

"Young lady," I glared, "you're going to have to get up and take a seat in the back. I cannot preach looking up the front of your dress!"

Not long after that, the same church invited me to speak on Ladies' Day, and I had discovered that my old *King James* said women were supposed to keep silent in church. It seemed to be just the topic for the occasion, and I laid it on them. Finally I summed it all up. "Women, be quiet!" It was as simple as that.

When I'd finished my sermon, one of the ladies got up to take charge and see that the offering plate got passed. I jumped to my feet. "Didn't you hear what I just said?" I roared. "Women aren't supposed to preach in church!" And out the door I marched.

The more I thought about things the more I concluded that women had a terrible problem with sin. All the problems that men had seemed to escape me for the moment. I could see all sorts of sin problems that Vivian had, including a big one called materialism. I moved from a place of just trying to live the Christian life before her to trying to point out where she was so far wrong. Needless to say, the fruit of the Spirit was not what that produced.

* * *

By the winter of 1971, I was getting close to graduating from Southwest Texas Junior College. The next time the editor of the school paper asked me to write a column, I wrote it from my new viewpoint.

In my classes, I had previously spouted off about how wrong

America was on every score and how hypocritical the establishment churches were, and the student body elected me president. Now when I defended Christian standards and talked about the existence of God, they seemed embarrassed by my presence.

Still, I was president of my class and showed up on the dean's list every semester, and because of that, I guess, the local Lion's Club invited me along with several others to speak at one of its meetings. I ended up giving my testimony, and the men listened and seemed to think it was okay, though maybe not quite what they were expecting. One of the gentlemen there asked if I would like to write a column for the local paper. Would I! Quite naturally, I chose my best topic for the column—women, and how they ought not to wear make-up. "If God had meant for women to have blue eyelids," I wrote, "He'd have created them that way!" I wrote another one later that was just as bad.

A few days later I got a phone call from one of the wealthiest men in Uvalde. He asked if I'd drop by his office when I had a few minutes. I was a little nervous about going because I figured he was going to get onto me about some bills that my daddy owed, or about something else I didn't know about.

On the appointed day I stood outside his office. Finally he opened the door and invited me into his office where he took a seat behind a desk that looked as big as a football field.

He smiled nice and easy, "Ben, I appreciate your coming by."

Motioning me toward a gorgeous leather chair, he sat back down behind his desk and began rummaging around in a bottom drawer as he talked. *Here it comes,* I thought. *He's got the goods on me, whatever it is.* Finally he came up with a book and held it in his hands for a second, a far away look in his eyes.

"I've read several of your columns in the paper lately," he said softly. "You've got talent and ability, and a life-and-death message. You may not have heard that my dad just passed away. Just before he died, he purchased this Bible."

His eyes misted over and he gently tossed the book toward me on the desk. "Preach the Word, Ben!" He almost seemed to be commanding me.

"Preach the Word!" he said again.

I looked down at the Bible. It was a *Thompson Chain Reference Bible*, red-letter edition—with tabs. A sense of awe swept over me. God cared about the little things in my life—even my desire for a certain kind of Bible. He hears and answers prayer. The wonder of it filled my head and heart for the rest of the day, and the wealthy man's parting words rang in my ears.

I desperately wanted to be productive in preaching the Word, but my track record so far was abysmal. I hadn't seen anybody saved through my preaching, no matter how hard or loud I preached. My wife seemed further from Christ than before I had been saved. I thought of my rigid, unyielding positions and negative, condemning sermons. I thought of the bored, stony faces of so many in the churches where I preached, but I thought more of the sick, the poor, and the worn-out ones.

"God," I whispered. "I asked You not to give me religion. I know You can do anything. I know preachers are supposed to help people. What am I doing wrong? What's missing?"

17

Reality

THE MORE I READ MY NEW *Thompson Chain Reference Bible*, with tabs, the more convinced I became that I had overlooked something about this business of being a Christian. Just looking at the life of Paul the apostle, I could see a big difference between his faith and mine. He was always in hot water of some kind. He was either being arrested or beaten or stoned or shipwrecked, but it didn't seem to make any difference. As soon as he got out of jail, or his back healed from the latest beating, or whatever, he started preaching again. He never seemed to have a doubt that he was on the right track and that he was onto something.

There was no doubt in my mind at this point that I had overlooked something, so I went through the Bible from front to back, this time looking for something *I* needed to know instead of what I could preach that somebody *else* needed to know.

By the time I got to the Book of Revelation at the end of the Bible, the only thing I could see I might have missed was that I hadn't been baptized. I knew it wouldn't do much good to talk to my daddy about it because he was a Methodist and believed that baptism by sprinkling did the job. It seemed to me that when those powerful preachers in the Bible were baptized, they found a lake or a river and got in it. Or if they talked about baptism, it seemed there was a lot of water involved. I got in my car and headed over to see John Corcoran.

"John," I said as soon as he opened the door, "I need to be baptized."

I guess he could tell by looking at my face that this was important to me. He opened the door wide and motioned for me to come inside.

"You haven't been?" he asked. When I shook my head, he seemed a little surprised. "I guess I just took it for granted that you had." He sat down opposite me and settled back in his easy chair. "Baptism *is* important, Ben—the Scriptures make it pretty plain."

We talked for a bit about how God seemed to move both internally and externally upon people. Most importantly, their hearts had to be changed. They had to be born again, made new internally by the Holy Spirit. But they also needed to take an external step, which in my case at this point was water baptism.

Jesus Himself told His followers that they were to make disciples *and* baptize them in the name of the Father, the Son, and the Holy Spirit.[1] It was internal and it was external.

Similarly, Peter on the day of Pentecost told his listeners to repent—change inwardly—and to be baptized; that is, show forth the change externally. Three thousand people responded. It was clear to me that I needed to do the same.

"Why don't we set it up for this Wednesday evening at my church?" John concluded.

I felt a lot better just knowing I had set a date to be baptized. When I left John, I thought, *This is Saturday. Four more days 'til Wednesday. Come Thursday morning, my life is going to be a lot different.*

At last the big night arrived. I was running a little late, so I loaded Vivian and the boys into the car, promising we'd grab a bite to eat after church. We drove to the little white Christian Missionary Alliance church on High Street for the Wednesday evening service. A small crowd welcomed us with open arms. They were all white, but I knew it didn't matter to them what color we were.

I enjoyed the singing, and I enjoyed the praying, and I enjoyed John's sermon.

After another song, John looked down at me from the pulpit and smiled. "We have Ben Kinchlow and his family visiting here with us this evening. Ben has asked to be baptized and I've made arrangements to do that tonight. We'd like for you to remain seated for just a few more minutes and share in this blessed time with us."

I got up and walked to the front and followed another fellow into a dressing room where I changed into some loose fitting clothes. Then he showed me a narrow little staircase leading down into a tank of water. Lights shined down on the water, but the church itself was dark. The man who had helped me dress touched my elbow, his face soft and kind.

"As soon as you see John step into the water," he whispered, "you can go on down."

I looked across the tank and saw John walking down another set of stairs on the other side and into the water. He bobbed a little, his white clothes spreading out in the water around him. He smiled across at me and held out his hand. Taking a deep breath, I stepped down, and gasped. The water was cold.

I made more waves than John because there was so much more of me, and when I looked down at John I began to feel a little nervous. There was a *lot* more of me than there was of John.

"Hold onto my arm, Ben," he whispered. "Just relax." He put a white handkerchief into my hands and put his left hand under mine. I could feel my heart speed up. "I'll place the handkerchief over your mouth and nose as I take you under," he said under his breath.

Then he stepped slightly to the right and a little behind me and prayed. "Ben Kinchlow, in obedience to the teaching of the Scriptures, I baptize you in the name of the Father, the Son, and the Holy Spirit. Amen."

He quickly covered my mouth and nose with the handkerchief and placed his right hand as far up on my shoulders as he could reach. The next thing I knew I plunged under water and surged right back up again. John wiped my face and beamed and shook my hand there in the baptistry. In the dark of the church, the audience started to sing, "Jesus Paid It All."

A lump the size of a hen egg swelled in my throat.

I could hardly talk as I changed back into my street clothes. I felt warm and loving inside. *This is it,* I thought to myself. *I'm going to give it all I've got—like Paul and Peter!*

When I stepped back out into the church, most of the people had gone. John was waiting for me, still grinning from ear to ear. Vivian stood over against the wall, holding a restless and wiggling little boy by each hand. It dawned on me that they hadn't had any supper. I hurried them out to the car.

"Hey, guys," I apologized, "you need food! How about some fried chicken?"

Levi and Nigel both frowned and started jumping up and down in the back seat. "Hamburgers! We want hamburgers!" One of them yanked too hard on Vivian's arm and she scowled and jerked his arm right back.

"I really would prefer Mexican food," she said tiredly.

Good grief! I thought. *I offer to take these guys out and what do I get? A bunch of argument!* Aloud I said, "Shut up! All of you! We'll eat cold sandwiches at home!"

"Aw, Daddy . . ." whined Nigel.

"You promised!" Levi pouted.

"You *did* promise," Vivian accused.

My insides churned. I not only had lost the warm glow of my water baptism experience, I felt almost as if I'd lost my salvation. I didn't care at the moment if I ever ate again. It looked as though I was right back where I started, water baptism or no water baptism.

* * *

From that night, a horrible thought ate at me, one I tried to knock down every time it stuck its head up. What if there really was no more to Christianity than sitting in a church pew or railing at people from the pulpit when you knew you weren't doing any better than they were, if as good? Suppose there was only one way to be a Christian—living with your family like everything was hunky dory, and yet knowing that lust hung on to the underside of your life like a parasite?

I reached the place where I felt if I didn't see my life line up with the life the Bible seemed to promise, I was going to give it up. I felt stranded in a no man's land. The thought of going back to where I'd come from almost strangled me, and I knew it was not an option, but I also knew I couldn't maintain the position I had reached, much less go on with God, as things were.

I reached for my Bible one more time, with an unspoken vow. "God, if *You* don't help me—if *You* don't show me what *You* want—I'm finished. I can't go on."

This time as I pored over the Scriptures, I took another look at Peter and Paul, and I discovered something I'd missed before. Sure, they were in hot water all the time for preaching the gospel. The only thing was, people were listening to them, and thousands were being saved. Another thing, no matter how bad things were, God either talked to them Himself or sent angels to tell them He was right behind them. The message was "Don't be afraid."

And those beatings and stonings—they didn't just get well; they got well immediately! I was face to face with miracles. But everybody I knew said those days were over. Today we just had to do the best we could with what we had to work with.

I closed my Bible and leaned back in my chair and stared off into space. "What if they're wrong?" I asked myself quietly.

* * *

Not long after that, I was given a book written by a fellow named Don Basham. In this book, Basham talked a lot about miracles he'd seen—just like Paul!

I was particularly impressed with one story Basham told about riding in the car with his wife while they were sulking after a quarrel. Basham began to "speak in tongues" and all of a sudden the car was filled with this radiant glow of beauty and he fell in love with his wife all over again. That sounded like manna from heaven to me. It sounded like God might have been listening—seeing my floundering and struggling, preparing to show me some answers.

I started reading everything on the subject I could find. Books began to turn up in the oddest places. John Sherrill's

They Speak with Other Tongues dropped into my lap from somewhere a few days later and convinced me that something called "the baptism of the Holy Spirit," along with spiritual gifts and miracles, was as much for our generation of Christians as for the first. According to Sherrill, it didn't make much sense to try to live the Christian life without it. I also gathered from Sherrill that the ones who worked the hardest in His church and did more of everything in general were the ones who had been baptized in the Holy Spirit and spoke in tongues. Right then and there I decided that was for me!

Not long after that I ran into a fellow in downtown Uvalde who actually had received this baptism and spoken in tongues. It amazed me. I felt as though I were talking to someone from outer space, almost like an angel. He told me about a book by an Episcopal priest, Dennis Bennett—*Nine O'Clock in the Morning.* I gathered from that conversation that Bennett had started speaking in tongues in his bathroom one morning at 9:00, so the next morning at 9:00 I went into my bathroom and waited—and waited. Nothing.

Something was happening in Uvalde, though. Where I had thought that maybe there was one person in town who knew about the baptism of the Holy Spirit and speaking in tongues, there turned out to be two. Then I met a third one, and pretty soon I found out there was this whole gang of them. The oddest thing of all was that most of them were some of the most prominent people in town.

Books on the subject passed from hand to hand like hot potatoes, going from one person to another as fast as they could be read. The one that struck me most was a book that described in detail how the writer had received the baptism of the Holy Spirit. It had happened to him when a visiting evangelist had prayed for him as he sat near a white brick fireplace in the white-carpeted living room of a prominent attorney. He had felt this warm glow begin in his stomach, rise up and fill his chest cavity and bubble out like warm honey in a flow of new words.

That's for me, I thought. *That's what I want.* I only had two problems: 1) where was I going to find a prominent attorney with a white fireplace and white carpet, and 2) how was

I going to get him to let me in his house? I may have changed, but Uvalde was still down South, and white lawyers were not in the habit of inviting black folks into their living rooms.

* * *

Shortly after that I was walking down the street when a shiny car that looked like it was a block long pulled up to the curb beside me. The window on my side slid down and I recognized another one of the wealthiest men in town. I knew he was worth several million dollars at least. But more important than that to me, I also knew he spoke in tongues. He leaned across the front seat and called my name.

"Hey, Ben! Got a minute?" He opened the car door. "Hop in. I'll give you a lift. There's something I want to talk to you about."

So I climbed into his shiny car and cruised off with him. "There's going to be a meeting at Taylor Nichols's house next week I thought you might be interested in. Fellow by the name of James Jones is going to be speaking on the baptism of the Holy Spirit. He's a good speaker. Traveling around the country having quite a ministry."

Several lights turned on inside my head. Taylor Nichols? A Christian attorney? No wonder my divorce proceedings had never gotten off the ground! Second, this Christian attorney was having a traveling evangelist at his house to talk to people about speaking in tongues. If I hadn't been invited, I would have crashed that party. Now if only he had a white carpet. . . .

The evening finally arrived, and when my wealthy friend picked me up, I felt as though something I'd been looking for all my life lay just around the corner. We pulled up to a big white brick house with a driveway curving in front and had a terrible time finding a place to park among all the other cars lining both sides of the street.

My new friend walked in without bothering to knock, so I followed close behind him. The living room was full of people, the den was full, up to and including the staircase, but I could see the top of a white brick fireplace across the way.

I immediately checked the carpet where it wasn't covered up by people. It was white. *This is it!* I thought, struggling to keep still. *This is it! It's gonna happen to me tonight!*

Brother Jones got up and started speaking and I thought he would never finish. Here I was ready for action and he was preaching! Finally, he got to the point.

"Every one of us needs the power of God in our lives," he finished. "The baptism of the Holy Spirit is for you, and you, and you. Many of you here in this group already know the joy and fullness of the Holy Spirit."

He paused as he waited for Taylor to put a chair in the center of the room. "We're ready to pray for any who would like to receive right now."

I was the first guy in the chair. "God," I silently promised, "If You just let me speak in tongues, I'll never ask You for anything else!"

All of a sudden, I felt somebody's hands on my head—several of them in fact. I thought, *I wish they wouldn't do that. White people are always wanting to see what black hair feels like!* Then I caught myself. "Oh, hey, I'm saved now." Everybody started to pray at once. "Lord God! We just ask You to baptize our brother, Ben, in Your mighty Holy Spirit. Lord Jesus, You are our baptizer, and You know Ben's heart. He wants to serve You more than anything! He needs Your mighty power, Lord. Just fill him now to overflowing."

I joined in. "Yes, Lord. Just give it to me, Lord!"

On and on it went, and finally the sound died down and I heard Brother Jones say, "Amen."

Amen? I thought. *You can't quit now! Nothing's happened! Where's the warm glow—the bubbling feeling?* I didn't feel a thing, but I looked up at the circle of expectant faces all waiting for me to do something and smiled a weak smile.

"How do you feel?" Brother Jones asked.

"Wonderful," I said. "Praise God, I feel wonderful."

Several other people were waiting for the chair, so I had to get up. But I really felt nothing had happened. I felt betrayed. I walked back to my chair smiling and nodding and sat there while they prayed for several other people to be healed or to have their legs lengthened or to be baptized in the Holy Spirit. All kinds of things seemed to be happening, but the longer I watched the more confused I got. Why hadn't it happened to me?

On the ride home I managed to make polite conversation,

but all I wanted was to get by myself and try to figure out what I had done wrong. The house was quiet, so I stretched out on the bed and stared up at the ceiling. It looked to me as though I'd done everything I knew to do. People were getting "it" all over the place, but I wasn't going to get it. Apparently this was for very select groups, mostly white, well-to-do ones. Was God prejudiced too? Wasn't I good enough? God didn't love me as I thought He had. Well, I was tired of the whole business. I had run up another rabbit trail, and I was worn out with hunting. The next day was Friday and I was due at work before dawn. I had to get some sleep.

* * *

The alarm snatched me out of sleep well before daylight the next morning. I headed out to the track and climbed into the big red bob-tail truck I was scheduled to drive. It carried a 6,000-pound load, and my job was to drive it back and forth over a mile stretch of sharp rocks to see what kind of wear the tires could take.

It was still dark, and the bumpy ride matched my mood. Now that I'd had a little rest, my feelings had changed from discouraged and worn out to mad—mad at God. Fed up. For the first thirty minutes or so I roared back and forth across the rocks, not sparing the horse power or my posterior.

Finally I thought, *I can't live like this. Baptism or no baptism, I can't live without You, Lord. But why—why didn't You give me the baptism in the Holy Spirit?*

Suddenly I found myself in a two-way conversation that took place partly inside my head, and partly with me talking out loud, and I knew only one side of it was coming from me.

"How do you know I didn't?" asked the other Person.

"Well . . . because I didn't feel anything—no glow, no warm bubbly—nothing!"

"I never said anything about warm bubbly."

"Oh," I said.

"I promised you you'd receive *power* when the Holy Ghost comes upon you."

"Oh," I said again.

"Did you do what you were supposed to do?"

"Yes, sir. As far as I know. I asked."

"All right, I did what I was supposed to do."

A surge of excitement shot through me, along with a new understanding. This baptism was mine—I had it!

"Okay, God, here's what I'm going to do," I said with my jaw set against the bouncing of the truck. "I'm going to open my mouth and I am going to start to speak. You are going to put words in my mouth, and whatever comes out is what I am going to say anyway! If it isn't anything but Thank You, Jesus! Praise You, Lord! Glory to God and Hallelujah! then that's what I will say."

So I opened my mouth to speak and my tongue crimped. It was a definite physical experience; my tongue crimped. And the next second, a beautiful foreign-sounding language poured from my mouth.

That's it! That's it! I thought, but I didn't dare stop or try to speak in English. Whatever it was, I was afraid if I stopped it wouldn't come back, so I kept on and on, bouncing back and forth over those rocks in that bobtail truck, speaking this strange but beautiful language. I was panting, running out of breath, so I grabbed the note pad I used to keep track of my laps around the track and tried to spell out the last word I had spoken, thinking that once I got my breath back I'd have a place to start up again.

Then the Voice in my head spoke again. "You don't have to do that." He somehow seemed amused. "It's yours to keep."

* * *

The world had actually taken on a fresh, clean look when I was saved. It was a tremendous relief to know I was saved from my sins, cleaned up and heading for heaven when I died. God had been very close that night when I had given Him my life. I knew He had been.

But with the baptism in the Holy Spirit, I became keenly aware of a dramatic difference. Where He had been close before, now He was in me, He was upon me, and I was in Him. And together we were in the Father, just exactly as Jesus had said it would be.[2] He had filled me, saturated me with His Holy Spirit; He had literally clothed me with power from on high.[3]

For the next few days after my baptism in the Spirit, the world looked as if it had been redecorated. I saw fantastic beauty in the littlest things—like the outlines of the leaves on a tree against a blue sky; they seemed sometimes to actually shimmer and sparkle, and it didn't matter whether the sun was shining or not. Now almost nothing I saw in nature slipped by me without my thinking, *My Father made that. Incredible! How could anybody not see it?*

In the past I had reached a place where nothing looked good to me, and I didn't enjoy anything I did. Now I got the biggest kick out of the simplest things—like the sound of my boys talking to each other in their beds at night, or the dimple in Vivian's right cheek when she laughed.

Along with all this, the Bible turned into a personal letter to Ben Kinchlow from Jesus Christ. All of it made so much more sense to me. I figured I might not be as brave as Peter and Paul—I sure wasn't looking forward to facing scourging or prison—but at least I understood now how they had done it. They were accustomed to seeing God *do* things—He was in control, and nothing could happen to them that He couldn't handle. It was a totally different thing from "religion" that just seems logical or comfortable as long as it doesn't cost too much. This was moving into an entirely different realm; being aware a lot is going on around us that most people never suspect at all.

The Bible became a gold mine of information about this invisible world and also about the visible one I lived in every day. I couldn't pass it by without picking it up. I had read the Old and New Testaments through more than once, but now almost everything I read took on a deeper, clearer meaning.

I found that if something was troubling me and I had been praying about it, a passage would almost lift off the page and take on a life of its own. It was uncanny. The words would fit my situation perfectly. I would know that the Lord was talking to me.

As time passed, I began to recognize when God was putting a thought into my head. This didn't happen overnight. I learned through trial and error to discern when it was He, and not merely my own mind. Today, I am embarrassed to remember some of the things I thought I "heard" from Him.

More often, rather than speaking audibly or lifting a passage of Scripture off the page or even injecting a sentence into my head, the Lord will reach me by causing me to *know* in my spirit that something is taking place. It will be simply a word of knowledge.

A new key in my life at that time was prayer. I loved to pray. I would spend hours behind the wheel of the cars out at the track, praying in English and praying in tongues. The sound of the tongues fascinated me, because it changed now and then; sometimes sounding heavy and Slavic, sometimes like Spanish or maybe an American Indian sound. Now and again it sounded so melodic and beautiful that I would weep with joy. That was another new thing—tears of joy that sprang up quickly and easily, where before I would have died rather than have anybody see me cry.

I began to love the dark of the evening or the early morning hours out on the track. Instead of being afraid to step outside the cars I drove, I felt drawn to get out under the stars and talk with the Father. I'd walk out in this big empty pasture, stepping around cactus and over dead stumps where rattlesnakes like to coil, and I knew there was nothing to be afraid of, not in life or in death. I had been given life on this earth by a powerful Father who loved me, and I would go to be with Him when I died. The in-between was just a blink of the eye compared to the eternity I'd spend with Him.

And finally, my preaching changed. I began to understand that if people could ever get an idea of how much God loved them and how much He could change their lives for the better, they wouldn't live the way they did, and they wouldn't be sleeping through sermons. I found myself caring about what was happening to them, listening hard to what they said, wanting the best for them. In short, I recognized that I had a new love for them; it was Jesus, in me, loving them.

From that point on, I felt a desperation about preaching. I *had* to preach. Everybody *had* to know, not only about salvation but about this incredible baptism in the Holy Spirit, but most of all, they had to know how much God loves them.

18

Learning and Serving

I FOUND OUT IN A HURRY that not everybody is waiting with bated breath to hear about the baptism in the Holy Spirit, especially the part about speaking in tongues. My dad was a good example. I was convinced he was the best man who ever lived, that he loved God, and there wasn't a doubt in my mind that he wanted to see me preaching the gospel in his Methodist church. But preaching the baptism in the Holy Ghost turned out to be something else again.

I well remember the day I broke the news to him that he'd been missing the boat all those years. (The baptism in the Holy Spirit does not necessarily endow one with great wisdom right away.) "I appreciate that you've been preaching all you know to preach, Daddy," I finished, "but you ain't got it all. You need the power of the Holy Ghost, and you need to be telling your people about it."

Instead of looking excited and interested, he looked tense. "Ben, that kind of thing has split more churches than just about anything else. It may be new to you but it's been around a long time. There's plenty of Pentecostal and Holiness churches around for those who believe that way."

He had a look in his eyes that made me think he was pointing me in that direction if I didn't straighten up. "Myself, I just don't see it for today. That was the way it had to be back when the church was getting started. The apostles had to have miracles to prove God was with them. Today we have the Scriptures to work with. We don't need miracles, and speaking in tongues just causes problems in churches."

For the first time in months, I felt anger begin to rise like hot steam from my neck to the top of my head.

"Don't need miracles?" I marveled, getting up and starting to pace the floor. "Daddy, don't you *see* the people sleeping in the pews every Sunday? Don't you *see* the fussing and fighting and running around that goes on in the families? Don't you *see* the sickness and poverty?! And we offer them *nothing* Sunday after Sunday!"

Daddy flinched at that and his jaw line set. "I've been preaching for years. You're telling me I've been giving the people nothing?" The look in his eyes said, "Be careful, Ben."

Mama came in from the kitchen wiping her hands on a towel. She looked worried.

"But," I slowed down a little, "there's so much more to give them!" I yanked a Bible off the coffee table and thumped it before shoving it at him. "It's all here—it's scriptural! The only way to get around it is to take the Bible and cut out Acts and 1 Corinthians!"

"How come so many reliable Bible commentators look at it so different from you?" Daddy argued. "I'm telling you, son, you're going to split the church wide open if you don't forget this tongues business!"

I was getting angry now. "Do you mean to tell me you're more worried about what happens to your little church than being true to the Word of God?"

I tossed the Bible back on the table and grabbed my car keys, heading for the door. "There's a *world* out there!" I roared, flinging the front door open and charging outside, Mama and Daddy both right behind me.

"Ben!" I heard Mama call after me. I kept going and scrambled into my old '59 Plymouth. I watched her turn toward Daddy. "Harvey, don't let him go off like that!"

I started the motor of the car and Dad's jaw line hardened even more. He turned to walk into the house and I laid rubber along the curb getting away from there.

I steamed most of the way home, but by the time I drove into our driveway, I realized I'd just lost the only pulpit I had to preach in. And I *had* to preach. I was on fire with the excitement of knowing that God is alive, and I wasn't much interested in doing anything but telling people the good news. I killed the motor of the car and sat there, staring into space.

After a few minutes, I made myself and God a promise. "If I have to preach in the streets, Lord Jesus, then the streets it is."

* * *

And the streets it was. Some of my new friends from the prayer group I'd joined offered to help with expenses, and in every spare minute I had after working hours, I concentrated my efforts on the teenagers in town. I was shocked by the condition of a lot of the young people I saw, even in small-town Uvalde. Most of them had long, straight hair—male or female. The macho man wore silk shirts, an earring and maybe a bracelet. The girls wore work shirts and blue jeans. Sometimes you couldn't tell the boys from the girls. "God," I prayed, "what is going on?"

"Look around and I'll show you," He seemed to answer. So I started watching what was happening in the homes. Most families spent their evenings and week-ends watching television. And of course, network TV never showed a solid male-female relationship with good, solid mother-father relations.

Then in real life, the daddy has often run off and left the family or been run off by the woman, or he's gone all day to work. The kids are left with a woman who gives the orders. The first authority figure most children encounter is a woman. When they go to school, who's the teacher? A woman. The bus driver? A woman. The crossing guard who represents the police in the eyes of the child? A woman!

Daddy comes home at night and the kids say, "Hey Daddy, can I go to the movies tonight? Can I use the car? Can Bobby stay the night?"

What does Dad answer? "Go ask your mother."

So the boys grow up thinking, "I can't wait to grow up and be a real man—like mama."

And the girls, watching the erosion of male authority, act more like men who are actually acting like women, who in turn are acting like men. It's easy to understand why so many young people turn to homosexuality as they try to figure out, "Who am I?" They watch their parents' marriages fall apart and their homes break up, and, with society telling them there's no God to call on, no absolutes, they take to drugs to dull the pain and to easy sex hoping to find "love" and acceptance.

Somehow, I knew I had to get to the kids. Maybe it was just as well that I didn't have a pulpit; the kids sure weren't in the churches. They were in the streets.

Since John Corcoran had moved from Uvalde to San Antonio, I turned even more to the men in the prayer group for support and advice. Most, but not all, were those wealthy white people who had prayed for me the night I received the baptism. Besides Taylor Nichols, I found a good Christian brother in Don Friend. He owned a successful automobile dealership with his brother-in-law, Frank Miller, who also became a good friend.

These men and their wives accepted Vivian and me wholeheartedly. We spent time together socially as well as in prayer and ministry. Vivian usually came along with me to these events, partly out of curiosity to see how these well-to-do white folks lived. For their part, they always welcomed us with open arms and seemed to assume that Vivian knew the Lord because she came along. Vivian never gave them any reason to doubt it. I prayed privately and fervently that Vivian would give her life and will to the Lord soon.

* * *

One evening, some of the men in the group took me aside after our usual prayer time.

"Ben," one of them began, "you need to be preaching full time." I nodded and said nothing.

"Furthermore," he went on, "we know that you've been preaching out at the college and around town." He paused, smiled, and then turned serious again. "I don't know if you realize it or not, but it's having an impact on some of the kids in town. They're listening." The other men nodded.

The fellow in charge of the discussion leaned forward, looking me right in the eye. "Brother, we really feel that the Lord has called us to help you in your ministry. Here's what we'd like to propose. We'll open an account at the bank and deposit money as long as the Lord leads. You can use it for whatever you feel like you need."

The next week, I went to see my boss at the track and told him I wouldn't be with them after graduation. I had to preach.

"Well, I think that's fine, Ben," he said, "but we hate to see you leave. We're beginning a new program here at General Tire—taking our brightest young men and sending them up to Akron to take a management training program. We'd like to be able to consider you for it."

"No kidding?!" I struggled for a split second. "I sure appreciate that. But I've made up my mind. I'm going to be preaching." I paused. "But, uh—if you don't mind I'd like to have you write me out a letter of recommendation just to have on hand." I mean, I was sold out, but just in case. . . .

So I left with a letter of recommendation. When I explained to Vivian that I had quit my job, she had somewhat to say about it. "You did what?!" she exploded. "And how do we get the bathroom floor fixed so the commode and shower don't fall through? When do we get decent beds for the boys so they don't have to sleep together on a roll-away? There's only so much we'll be able to do on my salary, you know!"

"Viv, you need to ask the Lord to forgive you for being so materialistic," I said, and like a "true spiritual giant," I walked out on the discussion.

I rented a building on the corner in downtown Uvalde where two main streets come together and called it "His Place." I taught the Bible, counseled, and talked with the kids and anyone else who wandered by. We saw an increase in the number who were being saved, but there were not as many as I would have liked.

Then I watched an amazing thing take place over several months. None of my friends knew what the others were depositing, and they never knew what my expenses were going to be. Yet, whether I spent $300 or $1,200 in any given month, that was always what turned up in the account. I felt certain I'd never again doubt God's ability to provide for me and mine.

I geared my preaching to the teenagers, and they began to come to listen. Often they stayed on to talk. I recall one boy in particular who came from a good church-going family, yet he was smoking dope and drinking and his parents had no control over him.

"What's the deal, man?" I asked him. I was discovering the kids didn't seem to mind straight talk from me, whether they were white, black, or Chicano. I knew there *was* a power working with me, way above what I could have done on my own. I sensed that the boy wanted to talk that night.

"What difference does it make how I act?" he muttered, wiping his nose. "I got saved a long time ago."

Well! I thought. *What have we here?* How could a saved person live the way he was living and think nothing about it?

"What are you talking about?" I asked.

He shrugged and grinned a crooked grin. "You know how it is. Once saved, always saved. What difference does it make how I live?" I had heard the theological arguments on that, but this wasn't theology—this was a young man's life, for now and for eternity.

I spent the rest of the evening explaining to the boy that we're saved not just for heaven but for *now* as well—that there's more fun and excitement in knowing Jesus Christ and living for Him than in a thousand "joints" or bottles of booze.

He listened, and his life was changed.

And so the kids kept coming, and more lives began to alter. I had a rapport with them because I "told it like it was," and loved them as they were, right where they were.

It was great to have a base of operations and a hangout for the kids, but the outreach was small, and the ministry was not having the impact I had hoped for. I felt there were many who wouldn't come inside a building, but who might listen to me if I just happened to be out where they were. So I planned an open air meeting in the Uvalde Municipal Park one evening, and invited a young man from the Baptist church to play the guitar for some singing.

We were all set up in the park and had a pretty good group

of thirty or so gathered around. I noticed one kid in particular who appeared to be far gone on drugs. He had a hound dog with him and looked as though he'd been on the road for a while. I started to pray silently for him.

Right at that moment, a city truck came around the bend of a road that encircled the park. A fog of insecticide poured from its tanks. The driver made his circle around the park, the fogger blowing the insecticide toward the middle where we were. We got it from all sides.

The weather was hot and uncomfortable anyway, with not a breath of wind blowing, and I could see that the choking, smelly stuff was going to roll over us like a heavy white cloud.

I turned to the guitar player. "Bob," I said, "if we don't do something, we're going to lose what little crowd we've got. They'll be gone and we'll never get them back together. We gotta pray!"

So the two of us dropped to our knees. I didn't have the nerve to pray out loud about the problem. Suppose I did and nothing happened? "Lord," I prayed under my breath with a whole lot less faith than the mustard seed the Lord spoke of, "we don't know what You're going to do about this, but You've got to do something or this meeting is going to be ruined!"

We got back on our feet with more resignation than expectation, and then watched incredulously as a slight wind stirred in the middle of the park where we were, and blew outward in all directions, clearing our area in a matter of minutes. I preached my sermon and we sang, and the hippie fellow with the dog came forward and prayed with me to receive the Lord. It was the only decision of the night, but to me, Billy Graham's giant crusades paled in comparison to that little meeting that night in the Uvalde Municipal Park.

Who said miracles were not for today?

* * *

After several months, it looked to me as if we might be set for life. But then, for the first time since the account had been opened, a strange thing happened. The funds from the group of men backing me seemed to dry up. There was no explanation. The money just stopped coming in as regularly as it had. I couldn't understand it. I knew God had called me to this. What was He doing?

Eventually Vivian and I were down to nothing and there was not even food in the house. She was scared, but she was also mad. She didn't understand this faith business and she didn't like to see her kids hungry. I left the house and drove aimlessly around Uvalde, wasting what little gas I had in my old car. It was a hot summer day, and the car didn't have any air-conditioning. Sweat dripped off my face.

I thought about going to Daddy, but I hadn't really talked seriously to him since the day I had stormed out of his house after telling him he didn't have all the spiritual power I had. I thought to myself, *He may not have all this power you got, Ben, but at least he's got a job.*

The more I thought about it, the more sheepish I felt about treating him the way I had. I knew if I went to him, he'd give me what I needed to put food on the table. I scrunched down in my seat, feeling sick at heart and foolish about the things I had said. I knew then that one day soon I'd have to go to him and make it right. But, for the time being, I had to get food for my family.

I turned the car around and started in the direction of Southside Grocery. I didn't know why. I didn't have any money in the bank. I had five overdraft notices in my pocket that Vivian didn't even know about. As I drove, I thought about the preachers I knew, and how most of them—except the big, flashy ones—didn't have any money. My own Daddy got paid $22 a week from his church, and had always been forced to work on the side to support us. I pulled into the parking lot at the grocery store and killed the engine.

"Okay, Lord," I said out loud. "I guess that's the way it is. Maybe preachers are supposed to be poor. It's okay if You can't support me; I'm not going to hold that against You. I'll never confess that You are not my Savior, and I'll still preach the gospel for You. But I can't stand to see my family hungry so I am going back to work for General Tire as quick as I can get there. That way You won't have the burden of supporting me."

I knew He was listening. I had that quiet feeling where

everything seems to hold its breath waiting for that still, small voice. I knew full well that if I wrote a check with the knowledge that I didn't have any money in the bank, I could go to jail. So I waited. Then a passage of Scripture came into my mind like a river overflowing its banks: "Faith is the substance of things hoped for, the evidence of things not seen."[1]

I had read that verse many times, but it had never been alive to me the way it was at that particular moment. I knew it was the Lord, and I knew what He was saying. I had what I needed in the bank account. It was already there.

And then I understood what the Lord was doing. He was teaching me not to rely on, or put my trust in, the men from the prayer group, no matter how godly they were. He was saying, "Look to Me. Trust Me. Have faith in *Me*, Ben."

I marched into the grocery store, grabbed a basket, and shopped for my family with abandon. I got everything we needed and some things that we simply wanted—even some fresh, hot barbecue. The bill came to something like $125, and I wrote the check with a flourish, secure in the knowledge from the Lord that it would be covered. I drove home without a worry in the world and when I started unloading those sacks of groceries, Vivian and the boys got excited. We had quite a celebration.

The next day I checked on my bank account and there was enough in it to cover the $125 check, including the overdrafts, and enough to last me for another two weeks. It seemed like great wealth at the time. I thought, *Man, this is the way to go! This ministry is about to move out full speed ahead. This faith business is all right.*

And then the still, small voice spoke again, the voice I had heard only the day before, "Now that you know who provides for you, Ben, it's time to go on to something else."

A word of caution may be in order here. I mentioned earlier that it takes time to learn God's ways and to know how He speaks and leads His people. Most of us make some mistakes along the way. But it is one thing to assume or presume God will do *what* we want, *when* we want it, just exactly the *way* we want it, and another thing to take an action in faith after He has given a clear, understandable leading that He will meet a genuine need or accomplish a specific thing. The first is presumption and the second is faith generated by a definite word from God.

The clearest instance given in Scripture of presumption is found in the account of the devil trying to tempt Jesus to throw Himself off the temple just to prove He was the Son of God. Jesus told him, "Thou shalt not tempt the Lord thy God."[2]

I didn't *presume* to write that check "in faith." I wrote with a supernatural measure of faith given by God as a by-product of His speaking that word from Hebrews 11. This was a rare and unusual instance in my life, and I would urge any Christian to move very carefully in this area, particularly in financial matters. The Holy Spirit is a gentle Person, and patient. We don't ever need to feel pushed or rushed into a hasty action that we will regret later, but it is also true that if God requires something, He provides for it. Put another way—what God orders, He pays for.

* * *

A week or so after the grocery store incident, Vivian had a piece of news for me. "The landlady's moving back to town and wants this house to live in," she said quietly. "We've got to find another place to live."

This new development caught me by surprise. Finding a place to rent that we could afford in a town the size of Uvalde wouldn't be easy. *Lord,* I thought, *Why this? Why now?*

And then a sentence from a week earlier echoed in my head: "Now that you know who provides for you, Ben, it's time to go on to something else."

Soon after that, the landlord at His Place decided he could no longer let us have the space, so there was nothing to do but close it down. When my folks heard about it, and about our house situation, they suggested that we move back in with them for the time being. An offer of a two-month job working in a fish hatchery came up, and we began a period of living one day at a time, taking each day's problems and each day's provisions as they came. Exactly at the time I got my first paycheck from the U.S. Government Fish Hatchery, I discovered all the money in the checking account to fund

His Place was gone. There had not been another dime deposited in it, and there never was again.

I was learning a lot, but it seemed like all ministry had come to a standstill. I could not for the life of me figure out what was going on.

Just before we moved in with my folks, a young man invited Nigel and Levi to go to a Vacation Bible School at the home of the man who had given me his father's Bible. Vivian was happy to have them busy for the morning and looked forward to some free time, but it turned out we all got a lot more than we bargained for. They came home all excited, both talking at the same time, and when we got them settled down, we found they had both invited Jesus into their hearts. It became obvious that, at ages seven and nine, they had met the Lord.

* * *

With "His Place" closed, and our landlady wanting her house to live in, we moved back in with my folks. They had a new home now, just across from the house where I had grown up. While I waited on the Lord to see where He was going to take us, I put in my time at the Fish Hatchery. It turned out to be like going to school, only better.

Part of my job was to take moss off the top of the pond and toss it up on the bank. The moss grows over the pool because the water is stagnant, and if it's not taken off, it uses up the oxygen in the water and the fish die.

One day I waded out into the three-foot-deep pool in my hip boots with a pitchfork and started raking the slimy stuff off the top of the water and tossing it over on the bank. The Lord started speaking to me in my head. "This is what I do with lives," He said. "Watch this." I took a forkful of slime and heaved it onto the bank, and just as the slime hit the bank, the Lord spoke again. "Watch!"

Out of the fresh pile of slime, a snake darted its head up and stopped still, looking in my direction. I stood there in the pond, leaning on the pitchfork. The snake looked like a stick poking up through the slime, and then I saw something just a foot or so away from him. It was a frog which the snake was looking to eat, but since it was the exact color of the terrain around him, the snake couldn't see him!

The Lord started speaking again. "I've made the frog that color to protect him. As long as he stays where he is, he's safe—he's resting under my protection."

For what seemed like several minutes, the snake didn't move, biding his time. After awhile, though, the frog must have grown tired of sitting still and he hopped just once. The snake had him in nothing flat.

The Lord drove His point home. "That's the way it is with you, Ben. As long as you rest under the shadow of My wings, you can never be touched. But the minute you move away from my protection, the enemy will have you just like that."

Yes, I could move away if I chose. God has given us free will. Satan is a defeated enemy, kept in check and on a short tether by the Lord, but we can choose to walk into his territory and risk the consequences. We can willingly go against God's will. We can choose to do things we know He doesn't want us to do. As Paul said, we can yield our members to unrighteousness or we can choose not to.[3]

Many people wonder why God lets us have that much freedom. The answer simply is that His kingdom is being built on love, not coercion. So He, the all-powerful One, lets us turn our backs on Him if we desire. But we will certainly suffer the consequences.

And so it went for the next two weeks. When the job was over I literally felt as though I'd been to a crash course in seminary, I'd learned so much about the Lord and His ways.

I had just cashed the last paycheck from the Fish Hatchery when Don Friend offered me a job managing a gas station he owned. I'd never managed a gas station in my life, and I wasn't crazy about having grease and gunk under my fingernails, but I jumped at the chance. And there in the service station in all that grease, I learned about human nature. And I learned about service and what the Lord meant when He said, "He that is greatest among you, let him be as the younger; and he that is chief, as he that doth serve."[4]

It was a good time, a time when I was absorbed in ministry

and growing in understanding of His ways, and yet I realized that I was once more beginning to avoid being outside in the dark by myself. I knew it was a thing I'd dealt with again and again, and it bothered me a lot that it kept cropping up, troubling me, sometimes taking the edge off the joy I'd come to know on a daily basis.

I knew the Lord wanted me to conquer it. Often He'd wake me in the darkest hours before dawn and nudge me to get out of bed and go outside into the dark to pray.

"Lord," I'd argue, "it sure is dark out there. Can't I just pray right here in the bed?"

"Outside, Ben," He would seem to say.

So I often spent time praying in the wee hours of the morning on the playing field at Robbs School, a new and integrated elementary school that had been built across the street from my parents' home. It was not an easy thing for me to do.

During this time, Harvey came home for a visit. I hadn't talked with him much in the months since I had come to Christ. He had always looked up to me as his big brother, and I had the feeling that he was watching me, to see if I turned into a Holy Joe or a religious nut who never got any pleasure out of life. I knew Harvey was running down and wearing out because I recognized all the symptoms—I'd been there before.

Finally, he was ready, and one afternoon in Mama and Daddy's living room, I led him to the Lord and watched as he received the baptism of the Holy Spirit. What a mighty God we serve!

* * *

I was overjoyed by what had happened with Harvey, and not long after that, someone who had heard about my ministry at His Place invited me to the Texas town of Del Rio to speak to a Bible study group. On the drive over, the Lord got around to the subject of fear in the heart of Ben Kinchlow.

As I drove down the highway, I was praying and really enjoying the Lord, so much so that I was almost oblivious to the world around me. But then I heard a sudden crash of thunder, and realized that rain drops were spattering against the windshield. The wind had picked up considerably. Glancing overhead, I saw an enormous, boiling black cloud approaching from the southwest, and in minutes, the drops of rain changed to blinding sheets.

"I'd better stop," I muttered, uneasiness creeping over me. I had slowed to a crawl and could feel the wind like a giant hand trying to push me sideways across the highway. "You can't stop," an inner voice argued. "Another driver coming from behind you could plow into you if you try it. You're going to get killed no matter what you do!"

Another voice inside me quietly insisted, "I'm not afraid. I'm a Christian." But at that moment, a clap of thunder sounded and the entire sky lit up with lightning, and I knew by the shape of the boiling black cloud that I was up against a tornado. Absolute terror washed over me. My arms and legs began to shake and I desperately tried to remember what I was supposed to do. The fear was so great that it was like being strangled, and I thought for one wild second that I would die if I didn't get out of its grip.

But then, like a great shaft of light shining down on another part of my inner self, I recognized a calmness, something close to joy. Outside, the wind raged stronger, sheets of water swept across the highway in front of me, and the fear remained alive and active. My teeth chattered, my breath came in short gasps, and my heart pounded, but the light and the calm and the joy stood its ground—a very clear division that amazed me. I could see and feel my fearing, trembling other self, but at the same time, I could feel the great peace and joy that had settled over the inner part of me.

At that instant I understood what was going on inside me. I clearly saw that the Holy Spirit is a real Person who comes to live inside Christians to free us, but that the flesh has a life of its own, too. There really is a division in a person who's been born again. His spirit has been brought to life by the Holy Spirit in a body where before only the flesh lived.

I understood then that as long as I lived in my human body I would always have a choice to make. I could choose to live my life after the flesh, or I could choose to live after the Spirit. The flesh is always there, ready and willing to take control, and Satan works on it and through it. But the Spirit of God is even more willing to live His life of peace and power in union with our spirit. "He that is joined unto the Lord is one spirit,"[5] and "God hath not given us the spirit of fear; but of power, and of love, and of a sound mind."[6]

I knew then that there would never be a time in my life when fear—or pride or anger or hatred, or a thousand other sinful emotions—would not try to leap up at times and take control. As part of the flesh or the "old nature," they are always ready. As the Bible says, "The flesh lusteth against the Spirit, and the Spirit against the flesh: and these are contrary the one to the other: so that [by yourselves] ye cannot do the things that ye would."[7] However, I could choose to "walk in the Spirit, and . . . not fulfill the lust of the flesh."[8]

If ever I was going to live any kind of a consistent life with God, I had to resist the flesh and recognize that God is God whether I always felt His presence or not. I needed to calm down and quit depending on my feelings to determine how things were going in my life because God has promised, "I will never leave you nor forsake you." I had seen Him move in miraculous ways too many times to doubt that He was working in my life. I had to learn to say "no" to my flesh—"I'm not going to be fearful, or angry, or doubting. I will keep my mind and my heart and my confession on Jesus, regardless of how things may look around me."

Outside the car, the wind had died to a standstill and the rain settled into nothing more than a shower, and when I pulled into the drive in Del Rio, I knew my life would never be the same again. I had quite a lesson to share with the Bible study group that day.

Later, on the drive back home, I saw trees and telephone poles that had been knocked over like matchsticks. The tornado had passed somewhere behind me while I had been driving through the rain and wind. My heavenly Father was still watching over me.

19

Vivian and the Lord

IT WAS A FAIRLY TYPICAL SUNDAY morning, this last Sunday in May of 1971. Vivian and I hadn't gone to church; we were planning to get together with the prayer group later in the day.

Vivian was watching a TV special on the Church of the Redeemer in Houston, a charismatic Episcopal church located in a formerly affluent area of Houston that had seen "white flight." The question the TV special asked was whether this kind of church can change and survive and minister in an area that was fast becoming heavily populated by Mexicans and blacks.

As I walked into the living room, Vivian snapped off the television set. "Why does the test have to be whether blacks and Mexicans move in?" she asked hotly. "I thought it was supposed to be 'whosoever will may come.'" She was obviously not in a particularly happy mood. I put on my best grin and started strutting and snapping my fingers. "Hey, baby, it's a gorgeous day, and it's time to hit the road for a picnic!"

The Texas Hill Country around Uvalde can be beautiful, especially in the spring after plenty of rain. Taylor Nichols and his wife had invited the prayer group to a Sunday afternoon picnic on a piece of property they owned along the

Nueces River. It was a gorgeous day, and the smell of barbecu-
ing steaks tantalized us all as we stretched out in lawn chairs
along the banks of the river.

Across the way on a rolling green hill, Levi and Nigel scam-
pered around and roughhoused with several other children.
I could see Vivian standing in the shade of a tall tree, talking
and laughing with some of the ladies. As far as I could tell,
she seemed to be having a good time. Looking over the twenty
or so people there, it dawned on me that one of the regulars
was missing. I glanced across at Taylor as he turned the thick,
lean cuts of meat over the grill.

"Where's Number 5 today?" I asked.

"He had an out of town meeting he had to make." Taylor
smiled his easy smile. "He sure hated to miss barbecued beef."

Don Friend stretched his blue-jeaned legs out in front of
him and surveyed the pointed toes of his cowboy boots. "I
don't know," he drawled. "I think he'd rather fly that plane
of his than eat—*any* day!"

Just at that moment, we heard the hum of an airplane engine
off in the distance. All eyes turned skyward.

"Here the rascal comes!" Don laughed, slapping his leg.
While we watched, the plane swooped down low and buzzed
over us. Levi's eyes just about popped out.

Frank Miller shook his head, chuckling along with the rest
of us. "Just couldn't stand to miss the party."

There was plenty of laughing and teasing that day, and
more good food than we could eat. It seemed to me, though,
that Vivian got quieter as the day wore on.

We had planned the day to relax and have a good time,
but there was more to it than that. Gus Fuentes, a local Uvalde
resident with a past that matched my own, had come to Christ.
After lunch, we gathered on the banks of the Nueces and I
had the privilege of baptizing him. I couldn't have asked for
a better day.

Vivian, however, continued to seem blue and sad, and was
ready to go home—"right now." Several of the ladies asked
if anything was wrong, but she couldn't tell them. I wondered
if she knew, herself. Levi and Nigel begged to stay and somebody offered to see that they got home later, so we made

our good-byes, with me laughing and making corny jokes as we got into the car. During the ride home, Vivian started to cry, and every time I asked her what was wrong, she just cried harder and said, "I don't know. I don't know!" I prayed silently in the Spirit all the way to the house.

It was mid-afternoon, and the house was silent and still. Vivian, still crying, went straight to the back bedroom and closed the door. Obviously she didn't want to talk. I was beginning to be a little peeved, so I picked up the Sunday paper and went into the front room. I relaxed on the couch, propped my feet up on the hassock, and started to read.

In a few minutes I heard the phone ring in the back room and I figured Vivian would answer it on the extension in the bedroom, so I didn't bother to get up. Suddenly, I thought I heard her cry out. I put the paper down and dropped my feet to the floor, listening.

There it was again. It sounded like she was talking to someone, but something was unusual about it.

"What's going on!" I muttered, getting to my feet. "Is she still on the phone?" I started down the hall, but then I heard peculiar sounds coming from the bedroom. I stopped in my tracks to listen. I recognized Vivian's voice, and realized she was laughing—or was she crying? Or both?

I reached for the knob and opened the door. She was sitting on the edge of the bed, doubled up, the tears streaming down her face.

I was still a little ticked that she'd made me miss the rest of the picnic. She had been blue and weepy all day and now, I thought, *she's having hysterics.*

"Hey," I said, "knock it off." I took her by the shoulders and gave her a good shake. "Enough's enough!"

She managed to nod her head up and down and then tried to tell me, "I'm not crying; I'm laughing." However, in that moment, there was no way I could understand her. She was speaking in a strange-sounding language. Then off she went again, falling back on the bed and shaking with laughter. She rolled over on her side and lay there giggling for several more minutes. Finally she sat up on the side of the bed, tried to wipe the tears off her face and grinned at me helplessly. Every time she tried to say something, the strange-sounding language came rolling out of her mouth.

In the space of that few minutes, I had experienced just about all the emotions. I had been angry, scared, bewildered, worried, relieved, and amused. And then came awe as I grasped what was happening to Vivian. In the past months, she had sat through dozens of prayer meetings and powerful messages, all my preaching and pleading, and now, somehow it had happened. She had been baptized in the Holy Spirit all by herself in the back bedroom of my parents' home. I was flabbergasted.

"Lord Jesus," I breathed, "You are something else!"

Vivian went on laughing and speaking in tongues until she finally broke through to English again. This had gone on for hours. We had arrived home about mid-afternoon. By the time she could explain to me what had happened, the sun had dropped below the West Texas horizon.

"It's *so* funny!" she gasped. "I was so scared—Ah, hah-hah-hee-hee-hee—how could I have been scared of the Lord? I'm so happy—so *happy!*"

She started to cry softly then, and laid her head on my shoulder while I held her close.

"I don't know why I felt so down all day, Ben, but when I got in here in the bedroom, one of the women from the prayer group called to see about me. She knew I was upset out at the land—she was so nice. She asked me if I thought it was the devil or the Lord trying to get through to me. It really caught me off guard. I thought about it for a minute and then told her I was pretty sure it was the Lord, and I started crying again. She said, 'We'll be praying for you,' and hung up.

"I dragged myself to the foot of the bed, and—I was so frustrated, wanting God, but afraid. . . . Finally I cried out, 'Lord, if You can use me in Your kingdom, let me know or else leave me alone!' And then. . . ." She turned to look at me and I'd never seen her so radiant, so beautiful. Her voice dropped almost to a whisper.

"Ben, He—He covered me with a beautiful, hazy film—almost like a *bride's* veil!"

"Praise You, Lord Jesus," I said loudly, and then we both slipped to our knees beside the bed and started praying together both in English and in tongues. Somewhere from the back of the house I heard a door open and figured my folks were home. For a split second I wondered if they were going to be tickled to death Vivian had been saved or put out because she was speaking in tongues. Vivian was off in her own world and if she knew the folks were home, she didn't care. A minute later I looked up to see Mama and Daddy standing in the doorway.

* * *

The folks didn't quite know what to make of all our experiences, but they let us do our thing. They knew the Lord had been listening to their prayers. He had let them live to see their two sons, a daughter-in-law, and two of their grandchildren saved.

From that point on, I had a new wife. She went through that wonderful honeymoon period with the Lord when the world turns brand new and shiny, and the Lord is so good to you you can't imagine you'll ever have another problem to face.

I've noticed He seems to operate that way. Right after a person meets Him in the baptism, He spends several weeks just letting them know He's around and showing them how much He loves them. Then, sort of like a child who has to be trained and taught, He expects His kids to begin growing up and learning His ways.

But for Vivian, that honeymoon period was extra special. She couldn't get enough of the Bible and suggested we start a Bible study in our home for friends and neighbors.

Shortly after she received the baptism, we got a call from her people in New Jersey. Her daddy was in the hospital and it didn't look as though he was going to live much longer. We knew our old car wouldn't make the trip and if it could have, we didn't have the gas money to go. Vivian walked the floor, her eyes brimming with tears, and every now and then she'd go and stand at the window and look out toward the northeast. I knew her heart was heavy, but there wasn't much I could do about it but pray. And when we prayed, we both felt the Lord saying the same thing. "This sickness is not unto death, but you should go to be with Vivian's people at this time."

"How, Lord?" I asked.

I got in touch with Taylor Nichols and Don Friend. They didn't bat an eyelash. Don lent me a used car off his lot to drive to New Jersey, and Taylor handed me his credit card. We started out on the trip but just twenty miles from Uvalde, I discovered almost by a miracle that the car had problems so I turned around and went back to the dealership. Don was out of the office by then, but Frank Miller was in, and he lent me another car—a nearly new Grand Prix. We were on our way.

At one point during the trip Vivian really cried out to God in prayer for her dad. As she prayed, she saw a vision of a man dying and she told me about it, her face the color of ashes. She was visibly upset.

"I don't understand, Ben! The Lord promised this sickness wasn't unto death!"

In New Jersey, we found things with Vivian's family pretty much the way they had always been. Vivian's dad was very sick with cancer, and her mother was extremely worried. I hated to see her so upset, because I felt she had always been fair to me. The lifestyles of one of her nieces, Annette, and her husband had us worried. Together with another nephew, they were heavily into drugs. When we slid the Grand Prix into a slot at the curb, they did a double take. "Man! You must have struck oil down there in Texas! Where'd you get a ride like that?" I explained it was on loan from a friend— a white man—and they thought I was putting them on. "Who you trying to kid?" They were openly skeptical. "What kind of a white guy is going to let a black use his Grand Prix to come all the way up here to New Jersey! Come on, get off my back!"

When I showed them the credit card too, they really listened. It gave us an opening for the two weeks we were there to talk about the Lord. It was hard to tell if they were listening at first, but Vivian went right on and told them what the Lord had done for her and they began to sit up and take notice.

As soon as we arrived in New Jersey, we went to the hospital and prayed for Vivian's daddy but his condition went from bad to worse. Remembering her vision in the car during the trip, Vivian agonized. "I don't know, Ben," she said. "I just don't know what to make of all this."

Neither did I, but a few days later, her father's condition improved dramatically, totally unexpectedly, and he was released from the hospital. And—equally unexpectedly—Vivian's brother-in-law died suddenly.

Before we left New Jersey to go back to Texas, I preached the funeral for Vivian's brother-in-law, and we shared Vivian's unusual vision with her family. This time when we talked about Jesus, they listened hard.

Shortly after we got back to Texas, Vivian's niece, Annette, got in touch with us. She wanted to know if she and her husband and two other of Vivian's nephews could come and stay with us for awhile, hoping to get their lives back in shape. We talked it over for a long time and Vivian and I prayed about it together. We knew it could be risky. Still, we knew these kids were in bad shape from drugs and heading for serious trouble if somebody didn't step in. We had the Bible study going at my folks' house, and we figured it might be a way to reach them. We said okay.

Soon we had two teenagers on our hands. We were especially concerned for Annette who was about twenty-one years old. Things had looked bad, and we knew the chances of her getting killed in the environment she liked to run in were great. She was so deep into drugs that the likelihood of an overdose was a real threat to her life as well.

The usual time came for our Bible study to meet, and she would attend. That particular night I taught from the Word, and we began to pray. You could feel the power of God very strongly in the room. I opened my eyes and felt impressed to get up and go pray for Annette. As soon as I touched her and began to pray, she started writhing in the chair and a different look came into her eyes. I knew immediately that we weren't dealing only with Annette. Somebody or some thing, evil, looked out of her body through her eyes.

It startled me. I shouted at the top of my lungs, "In the name of Jesus, come out of her!"

She stiffened and let out an unearthly scream that made the hair stand up on the back of my neck. At this point, I was acting on spiritual instinct rather than any previous experience with demons, so I yelled almost as loud as the demon. "I said—in the name of Jesus—*leave!*"

The other people in the room looked about ready to leave, themselves, and the girl stared at me with a wild, pleading look for just a second. Then she slumped in her chair almost as if she had fainted. She started to cry, and when she finally looked up at me, her eyes were clear, her face smiling and bright.

Today I know that you don't have to yell at demons to get rid of them. They just have to be told with the authority of Jesus that they must come out of a person. But I was learning then and I was taking no chances.

We had talked about demons in our prayer group, but nobody in the room, including Vivian and me, had ever seen anything like this before. Folks were dumbfounded, and even more so as the days went by and we saw our niece change before our eyes into a happy, healthy young woman.

* * *

We had been living with my folks now for several months and I was working for Don Friend in his automobile dealership, cleaning up new cars and getting them ready for the showroom. I appreciated the job immensely, and I was happy to be about my Father's business, teaching and preaching in every spare minute, but eventually I began to feel the pressure. One day at work, I talked it over with Don.

He started digging in his pocket and brought out his money clip. "There's a retreat going on up at Mo Ranch near Kerrville. It's called a Camp Farthest Out." Don stripped a $100 bill from his roll and handed it to me. "Take a few days off. Take Vivian and the kids. Relax and spend some time with the Lord. You can take my wife's car." He handed me a set of keys and gently shoved me out the door while I tried to thank him.

It was late fall, and the trees along the highway ranged in color from bright orange to golden yellow. Vivian and I drove the two hours to Kerrville, soaking up the peace and quiet and the beauty of the countryside. Leaving the main highway, we entered a paved road and then followed a driveway to several rock and stone buildings that make up Mo Ranch.

We walked to the registration building and a barrel-chested fellow and his tiny little wife reached out to hug us before we could even tell them who we were. That kind of thing continued for the three days we were there. We never went to a single meeting that one of the fellows, along with his wife, was not waiting at the door to hug us.

We met mornings and evenings for worship and praise, and then heard a top-notch speaker each time. It was the first time I'd ever been with that many people who were that crazy about Jesus. I ate it up. The boys had plenty of supervised activities and things to do, so Vivian got a good rest, too.

At one of the meetings, a little, dark-haired, dark-eyed fellow named Bob Bearden stood up to tell about this ministry he had for drug addicts at a place that he called Christian Farms. At first he struck me as busy—nervous, almost. He seemed to be having a hard time standing still. But the more he talked about his work with addicts, the more interesting he became.

"There *is* a cure for drug addicts!" he insisted. "Jesus Christ is the answer and He is able to set them free instantaneously! I've seen Him do it time and again." After the meeting I had just a minute to shake hands with him.

That evening after supper and before the meeting started, Vivian and I took a walk around the grounds of Mo Ranch. The buildings were old, but they looked as if they'd be there forever—solid rock, with big dark wood beams exposed on the inside. It was rustic, but big and comfortable.

We ambled hand in hand around to the back of the buildings and across a wide lawn to stand on the banks of the river that flowed along the back of the property. It had been a fantastic week-end. What a contrast to my former idea of a great time! It was clean, it was sane, it was wholesome and it was rich with meaning; and come Monday morning, there wouldn't be any hangover to deal with. We hated to see it end. Then I had a bright idea.

"Hey! We haven't spent nearly all of that $100 Don gave

us. If we get an early start tomorrow morning, we could drive to Houston and take the kids to see the Astrodome before we head home. What do you say?" She didn't need much persuading, so early the next morning we said good-bye to the new friends we'd made at Mo Ranch and headed south.

In Houston we wandered around the big sports arena called the Astrodome, still relaxed and enjoying ourselves. We decided to have some fried chicken before heading back to Uvalde.

As we were leaving, Nigel tugged on my shirt. "Daddy, I feel sick at my stomach."

"Okay, pal," I said, "we'll make you a spot in the back of the car and you can lie down on the ride home." We managed to get him out of the door of the restaurant and into the driveway before the first deluge of vomiting hit. It was like nothing we had ever seen before—a projectile type of vomiting that just went on and on until he had nothing left in his stomach, and still he went on retching.

Vivian got into the back seat with Nigel and stretched him out on the seat with his head in her lap. "He's clammy, Ben!" She looked at me, and I knew by her expression that she was scared. The next minute, Nigel's eyes rolled back in his head, and I thought, *He's dying! What am I going to tell his grandmother?! I've taken her grandson off on a pleasure trip and killed him!* Then a thought came into my mind. *Prayer for Nigel!* We needed prayer, and the only church I could think of that I felt sure could pray effectively was the Church of the Redeemer.

"Church of the Redeemer! It's in Houston! We'll take him there and they can pray for him!" Before Vivian could answer I started the car and tore out of the parking lot, driving like a mad man through the traffic. Then it dawned on me that I had no more idea than a jack rabbit where the Church of the Redeemer was.

In the back seat I heard Nigel moaning. "Mommy, Mommy, it's getting black!"

"Oh, God!" I slammed on the brakes at a phone booth and yanked the door open, frantically thumbing through the big directory looking for the Church of the Redeemer. I dropped the book and had to start over again, but finally found the number I was looking for. My hands were shaking so badly I could hardly get the dime in the slot, and then I dropped the phone and by the time I got it back to my ear I'd forgotten the number. Out in the car I could see Vivian rocking Nigel and feeling his forehead. Near to tears, I started looking for the number again, but then a peculiar thought came into my head.

"It doesn't have to be the Church of the Redeemer. It doesn't have to be a charismatic church—just *any* church where there are believers will do. 'For where two or three are gathered together in my name, there am I in the midst of them.' "[1]

I ran my finger down the list of numbers and stopped at the first church I came to. While I dialed the number, fuller understanding came to me.

"Lord, You're no respecter of persons and it doesn't have to be the Church of the Redeemer. There aren't any special, select churches with You. You're the One who does the miracles . . . ." I looked out toward the car and realized Vivian was smiling and waving at me. I threw open the door of the booth.

"What is it? What's happened?"

"He's okay," she said softly. "He's all right." By the time I walked back to the car, Nigel was sleeping peacefully on the back seat of the car. I slipped behind the wheel, and sat for a minute, pulling myself together, trying to grasp all that had been going on besides Nigel's food poisoning.

I was certain God had taught me something in this experience that I needed to remember. "Don't ever think there's only one certain place or one certain person where you can get help when you need it. The power is in Me, not in people or places." And since that day, I've never made the mistake of putting my trust in any one man or institution.

* * *

Not long after the week-end at Mo Ranch and our trip to Houston, I woke up one night out of a sound sleep, and I knew the Lord was calling me to get up, get dressed, and go outside to pray. When I looked out the window, it was black as pitch, without a trace of light from even a star. It couldn't have been later than 3 or 4 o'clock.

Lord, I thought, *it sure is dark out there. Can't I pray right here in the bed?*

I already knew the answer, so I dressed and slipped out of the house without waking the family and walked down and across the street to the playing field of Robbs School. I began to thank Jesus for His love and mercy, and then I felt myself being drawn into His presence. Falling face down in the grass, I must have spent more than an hour in prayer, knowing that I had broken through to the throne room of God.

I found myself marveling at what God had done in my family, and then I flashed back to my past and remembered all the pain and rage and bitter hatred that had dogged my life for so many years. Now there was love and laughter in my house, and friends were around me who were as close as brothers.

Face down there on the ground I praised God for His incredible goodness. When I ran out of English I rejoiced in tongues, listening in wonder at that marvelous gift. This was actually the Spirit of the living God speaking through my lips, using my tongue. It was as if I were standing aside in awe, listening to God talking to God!

"I *love* You, Lord!" I cried out loud into the dawn. *"Thank You, Jesus! Thank You!"*

And then I heard a sound—a horrible, snorting sound from something alive. My scalp prickled and I jumped to my feet and stood for a second, not breathing, fighting for control, but fear broke loose and tore at me with all its might. I spun around and ran.

I hadn't gone more than a few steps when I saw the dark outline of a horse, snorting and ambling along a fence near the school yard.

"Oh, God!" I cried out, embarrassed at how I'd acted in the presence of Almighty God after all He'd done to show me His love and power. "Father, I've blown it again, and I ask You to forgive me. I learned that day on the way home from Del Rio that I may run around like a chicken with its head cut off, but You don't. And I know You don't love me

any less for this." I leaned against the brick wall, trembling
and dejected, and then at this weak point, the Lord spoke.

"Isaiah 51."

"Isaiah 51?" I didn't have any idea what was in Isaiah 51,
but I spun around and headed back to the house, closing the
door softly to keep from waking the family. Flipping on a
lamp, I grabbed my Bible from a table and dropped into the
nearest chair.

"Hearken to me," I read, "ye that follow after righteousness,
ye that seek the Lord: look unto the rock whence ye are hewn,
and to the hole of the pit whence ye are digged. Look unto
Abraham. . . ."

Look unto Abraham. It seemed almost like a command. I
turned back to Genesis 12. "Now the Lord had said unto
Abram, Get thee out of thy country, and from thy kindred,
and from thy father's house, unto a land that I will shew thee."

I dropped the book into my lap, heart pounding, excitement
kindled by what I'd read. He had described my position exactly. I was in my country, Uvalde, with my kin folks, and I
was living in my father's house. I knew immediately what
the Lord was saying. It was time for me to leave and get
out of that situation. The only question was, where were we
supposed to go?

The next day at work, I talked the situation over with Don
and Frank. "I know now, for a fact," I said, "that the Lord
is calling me away from Uvalde. He has told me to leave
my father's house and kindred and go to a land that he will
show me. I just don't have any idea where that is."

The two looked at each other and seemed to be deep in
thought. Finally Don spoke. "I wonder if you shouldn't get
in touch with Bob Bearden? I know he's hosting a drug rehabil-
itation meeting going at Fort Hood in Killeen." Reaching into
his pocket, he grinned and handed me a set of car keys. "Take
my wife's car."

* * *

The Fort Hood drug conference turned out not to be just
a cut and dried military presentation, and afterward when I
talked to Bob Bearden, he certainly was anything but cut
and dried.

"Listen, Ben," he said, changing his position and running

his hands through his hair. He pulled at his lower lip and straightened his collar. "I think you and your wife ought to drive out to the farm while you're in the area. You can look it over and see what you think. It's not far from here. Why don't you meet me there in a half hour or so?"

Vivian and I took Bob's directions in hand and drove out to take a look at Christian Farms. We followed the directions to the letter, but they kept leading us to this rundown set of buildings standing almost out in the middle of nowhere. We circled back two or three times, looking for this forty-acre farm Bearden had talked about with all that enthusiasm. Finally we pulled up and I killed the motor in the yard of the first ramshackle building.

"Looks like this is it, Baby," I sighed. I'd be polite to Bob Bearden and Don Friend, but there was no way I was going to stay in a place like this.

"Oh boy!" Vivian breathed.

"No *way!*" I said, slowly getting out of the car and walking up to the porch.

20

Drug Addicts

I STOOD THERE WITH ONE FOOT on the step and one on the porch. There didn't seem to be much activity. I stepped up to the door and knocked twice. A minute ticked by before I heard a shuffling sound approaching the door. It creaked open and a dirty, long-haired, skin-and-bones young man blinked against the sunlight.

"Hey," I said, feeling as though I were too loud, but at the same time wondering if he could hear me. "I'm looking for Bob Bearden. This isn't his place, is it?"

I still had hope. The guy wiped his arm across his nose and sniffed. "Yeah, but he's not here right now."

I glanced at my watch. "Well, I had an appointment to meet him here around three. I guess he's running a little late."

The fellow shrugged, and stood there like a robot. I could smell everything from dirty hair to dirty feet, but the empty, desolate look from behind the round-rimmed glasses went through me like a rusty saw. He couldn't have been more than twenty and he was already burned out.

He seemed to rouse a little. "Wanna come in and wait?" he asked.

"No, thanks," I answered. "I think I'll walk around the grounds 'til Bob gets here."

I walked slowly back to the car and stuck my head in the window. "Viv, Bob's not here yet, but he should be along pretty soon. If you don't mind, I think I'll just take a look around."

She pulled her sweater over her shoulders. "You can *look* all you want to."

I walked across the yard to a pasture and stooped to crawl through the barbed wire fence. Hands in pockets, I listened to the quietness around me and thought, *Guys that have been into drugs need this kind of fresh air and peacefulness—miles away from the nearest pusher.*

I walked out across the open field and topped a small, grassy rise where I could look down on the "farm." There wasn't an animal in sight. "I thought farms had animals."

Looking down at what I guessed was the main house, I doubted if it had had a coat of paint in fifty years. It looked as old and tired and worn out as the young men Bob Bearden had described who came to his drug program from Fort Hood. Drugs. One of Satan's best tools. I felt my throat tighten and hot tears welled into my eyes.

"Lord Jesus," I started to pray. "Is this it?"

"This is the land I have shown you."

"What about Vivian and the boys? How can I ask them to live in a place like this?"

"Look behind you."

I turned and looked back at the barren, ugly line of old buildings and dirt yards. The Voice went on speaking inside my head. "When you leave, those buildings will be painted white. There will be a red barn for cows, and fenced pens for pigs. White chickens will run loose in the yard and healthy, healed young men will tend to them."

"Yes, Father," I said, bowing my head. "Yes, Father."

* * *

It had been easy enough to say yes to the Lord that day up on the grassy knoll with the feeling of His presence strong around me and His words ringing in my head. Persuading Vivian that I really had heard from Him was another proposition altogether. Bob Bearden had come up with a plan that made it a little easier to get her to agree to move out to the farm.

"Ben, I can't afford to pay you but a hundred a month right now," he said, running his finger inside his collar and tucking his shirt under his belt. "But you can live here on the farm and I'll be sure there's plenty for you and your family to eat. Then there's this other thing that might work out. I think we might use your street experience with addicts as credentials to get you officially registered with the drug program over at Fort Hood. I think we can get you a GS-11 rating with the government, which would mean at least a $12,000 yearly salary. Maybe as much as $18,000."

I tried to be indifferent—I wanted this to be by faith, for God—but I couldn't help thinking how nice it would be to have a salary like that to live on. There wasn't any way that Vivian could work since we'd be living so far from town. Besides, I had a sneaking suspicion she was going to have her hands full just getting the house fit to live in.

So I broke the good news about all this money we were going to make. It was not so much the question of having enough money at Christian Farms that bothered Vivian. She had been through so many of my grand schemes that she was rightfully skeptical. It seemed to me that the stability of a government job was something we both needed. She got busy and sold or gave away nearly everything we had so it would be easier for us to move. We loaded up what was left in a borrowed Chevy van and headed for Christian Farms.

For the first two weeks after we moved in, Vivian cried every day. Every day. I thought she would never stop. I understood that she had good reason to cry, but I couldn't see how it helped our situation. And we did have a situation on our hands.

We moved into the same house where these supposedly "recovering" drug addicts had been living, but they had been left with absolutely no supervision. It's hard to describe the level to which drugs can take a person. For example, these young men and women simply did not bathe. And they would vomit and lie in it or shuffle off and leave it. Once in a great while they made a half-hearted attempt to clean it up. If they couldn't make it to the bathroom in time, then they left their ruined clothes on the floor or kicked them in a corner if they had clothes to change into. The smells in the house nearly turned the air green.

So Vivian scrubbed and cried and cooked and cried and scolded and cried while I tried to find out how to make a farm work. And in the meantime, we waited to hear whether my government salary was going to be $18,000 or only $12,000.

Nigel and Levi took to the farm like a sick kitten to a warm brick. The addicts seemed to brighten a little when the boys were around and they got to where they teased and rough-housed with them some. I watched my boys roam the fields and swing from the trees and eventually chase the chickens and decided that farm life might not be all that bad. Maybe I could make it work after all.

The chicken situation looked like the simplest place to start, so Bob went out and bought some first thing. I went down to the hen house to talk things over with them. "The boss says you girls should have laying mash to eat. That's fine and dandy. You get your laying mash just as soon as you start laying eggs!"

One day after the chickens—white leghorns—arrived, Bob Bearden showed up at the farm to see how things were progressing. "How many eggs are you getting each day?" he asked, scratching the back of his neck and pulling on one ear lobe.

"Man," I said disgustedly, "them chickens ain't laying *nothing!*"

"Well, are they getting plenty of laying mash?" he asked.

"Absolutely not!" I assured him earnestly. "They're not laying enough eggs to pay for any laying mash!"

I believe that's one of the few times I ever saw Bob Bearden stand perfectly still.

Then there was Hope, the cow we bought from a local Baptist preacher who couldn't find enough good things to say about her. "She's just the gentlest, sweetest, most loving cow you could find anywhere. We just weaned her calf, so she's giving plenty of good milk. She's been bred so she'll be calving in another few months. You ought to have plenty of milk for everybody on this farm for at least two years."

I couldn't wait to tell Bob about my great bargain—until

that evening when one of the guys tried to milk her. We found out Hope kicked like Lou "The Toe" Groza.

A couple of days later, Mama and Daddy drove up from Uvalde for a visit. I was really tickled to see them, since I knew Daddy was an old cowhand from his days of working on ranches and at the dairy.

"We got this problem, Daddy," I told him as we walked together out to the barn. "We got this heifer and she kicks the daylights out of anybody that tries to milk her."

He chuckled and shook his head. "Aw, Ben, you just gotta know how to handle 'em." He walked up to Hope, who was in for the evening, and drew up a milking stool. "You got to put your head right here in her flank so she can't get her leg up." He reached for the bucket.

"Daddy, I'm telling you, that cow kicks!" He just smiled and laid his head right in her flank, and in no time at all, he found himself resting up against the side of the barn.

After that, Daddy showed us how to slip up on Hope's blind side and tie her legs together at milking time, and we did manage to get what we wanted from her.

With Hope and the leghorns under control, we added a sow to the farm and named her Charity. She indeed turned out to be more charitable than Faith and we soon had a blessed event. Levi and Nigel had the time of their lives playing with those little pink piglets when their mama wasn't looking. We all suffered through a failed effort at "faith healing" when one of the piglets got sick and died in spite of much laying on of hands and the prayer of faith.

* * *

The men who had come or been sent to the farm seeking help seemed to benefit from working with the animals. They also enjoyed our youngsters, and these diversions allowed me to get to know them and gain their confidence. Vivian had all she could manage just keeping the house going, and she didn't have a lot of help with cooking for all of us.

One day I got a call from Bob Bearden to come to his house as soon as possible. I found him talking and working with a young fellow who was hooked on heroin, but desperate to get the monkey off his back. We talked with him about Jesus and the power He had to set him free and the guy listened intently.

Finally, Bob and I laid hands on his head and prayed for him, first binding Satan and commanding him to leave the boy alone, using the authority of Jesus Christ. We joined in prayer and, when we finished, the boy's eyes were clear, his hands were steady and his face beamed with a smile.

Most psychologists, sociologists, and physiologists tell us it is impossible for a heroin addict to withdraw without going through torture. But this boy had no discomfort and was immediately free of his addiction. My confidence in God's ability to handle any situation soared as I watched this young man stabilize and eventually go out to stand on his own. Unfortunately he didn't stay grounded in God and fell back. Yet there is no question but what he was cured at that instant.

I was tremendously excited about the potential there at the farm, and at this point Vivian looked as if she was going to be able to take it, but it was still touch and go. Shortly after that, I walked into the kitchen one afternoon and found her sitting at the table, tears flowing.

"Aw, Viv," I began, but she gave me a look that stopped me short. This time, it was more than just the farm.

"Mama's sick," she said. "It's really bad. They think I'd better try to get to Jersey right away if I want to see her again."

Money was a problem—real cash money—but somehow we got it together and sent her up to be with her mother. I hated to see her go because I almost wondered if she'd be coming back. I knew something had to give. The night she left, I called the young men there at the farm to a meeting.

"Listen, you guys," I began, "if we don't make some changes around here, I'm not sure the Kinchlows will be around much longer. I'm not even sure Vivian is going to come back to this place."

The look on their faces surprised me, but their reaction the next day was even more surprising. They swarmed over the place like gangbusters, cleaning it out. They filled holes and cracks in the walls, and slopped paint all over the place, and when the dust settled, the whole house sparkled—repainted from top to bottom, inside and out.

The day Vivian came home was special. She had lost her Mother, so her emotions were tender, and she was very nearly overcome when it sank in on her that these young men had come to care about us as people.

After that, Vivian really threw herself into the work of the farm, and spent time counseling with the girls who came out to help with the cooking. She got a small inheritance from her mother and used the money to buy a few pieces of furniture for the house and generally seemed happier than she had been in months. She was amazing. Her "Hopping John"— a black-eyed pea dish—became a legend in its own time.

Then just when she was going great guns, she began to feel queasy in the mornings and drowsy all day long. About the time I got word I had been turned down for my GS-11 job, Vivian went to the doctor and learned for certain that she was pregnant with our third son, Sean. I remembered her terrible fear of pregnancy and expected her to be devastated, but she surprised me. Once she got over the shock, she seemed pleased. As far as I was concerned, a baby in the house would be great, but I also knew there had to be more money coming in from somewhere.

I found a part-time job as a bus driver and study hall teacher for the Killeen school system; the salary totaled $100 a month. Life was not easy, but it was good.

We continued to see significant change in the lives of the young men at the farm, and it became commonplace to see newcomers delivered from narcotics. They took their place with the others as long as they needed time to get their feet on the ground, working at the farm and studying the Bible.

On Sundays, we crowded into the van and drove to the local churches, including the African Methodist Episcopal Church, where I was eventually ordained, and was later assigned to preach at two small country churches each week. People in the community became involved in the ministry as well.

Before long, people began inviting me to speak, and eventually a chapter of the Full Gospel Business Men's Fellowship International out in West Texas asked if I would come. I checked our financial situation and discovered I had two assets—a $20 bill and a tank full of gas in my car. I agreed to go.

There's a big difference in my part of Texas and West Texas. Out there, the spaces sit next to wide open spaces and most of the trees along the way are small and scruffy. The wind is nearly always blowing and it seemed to me that a haze of dust always hung in the air. If you're used to trees and hills and grass and gentle breezes, that part of Texas can make you feel a little forlorn, especially at night. It can be a long way between gas stations.

So off I went with my full tank of gas and my $20 bill, and I made the trip there just fine. As long as I held on to that twenty for the trip back, I didn't see any problem.

The meeting ran late and I gave my testimony and preached my sermon on God's grace and His ability to meet every need and sat down. Then the treasurer got up and said it was time for the offering and explained what their needs were and how much good they could do with the money.

"Just pray," he finished, "and ask the Lord what you ought to give."

"Too bad I can't give anything," I said to myself. "All I have is $20 and it's probably going to take me $12 or $15 of that just to get back home."

Everybody started praying, so I joined right in. "Lord, I really praise and bless You. Thank You, Lord Jesus. Hallelujah. Glory to God. Bless this offering, Lord!"

Then I heard the words: "Give the $20."

I stopped. "Where'd that come from?! That can't be God! I can't do that! It's all I've got!"

Then one of those two-sided conversations started up in my head.

"Give the $20."

"I'm sorry," I pleaded. "I can't," I cajoled. "I'm not," I rebelled.

And I didn't. I put my hands in my pocket and held onto that $20 for dear life. The collection plate passed by and I sat there thinking, "I'm sorry. I can't give all I've got and be out here in the middle of nowhere with nothing. If I do get anything, it will be a check and I can't cash a check in the middle of the night."

The meeting ended and I stood at the door shaking hands and nodding and smiling and feeling a little guilty about the offering but enjoying all the good fellowship. A little insignificant looking guy with a round face and glasses and thinning hair walked up to me and shook my hand. I felt a piece of paper pass from his palm to mine and he turned and walked away before I could say anything. I slipped the paper in my pocket and after the crowd had thinned out I went to my car to head home. Under the lights in the parking lot I looked at the paper the little fellow had pressed into my hand. It was a brand new $100 bill.

Instead of feeling elated, I was sick at heart. I turned on my heel and ran back into the building and could hardly wait to give the $20—but not the $100—into the offering plate, and I knew I'd failed the test and missed the blessing. Instead of being able to shout praises all the way home because I'd heard the Master's voice and done what He told me *when* He told me to, I felt like a whipped puppy with its tail between its legs.

I realized that night that I had been thinking of myself as getting from the kingdom of God rather than giving. Jesus had let me get by with that for a long time and blessed my efforts to serve Him in spite of it. But I knew that night that it was time to learn a new thing about God and the way He works with His people.

Whenever He asks us to do something, He's already made provision for it. We're not to be afraid to trust Him. We have to come to the place where our hands are open before Him, never closed. How can God slip money or anything else into a clenched fist? We have to learn to be willing to give Him the best at the beginning, because whatever it is we are holding onto, it can't begin to compare with what God has waiting for us. Furthermore, God has not only prepared in advance for what He asks us to do, but He also will multiply back whatever it is that He asks us to give—$5 \times 20 = 100$; what bank gives that rate of return on an investment?

Of course, I made it back home from West Texas to the farm in great shape, except for a bruised conscience.

* * *

The little grassy knoll overlooking the farm had almost become my prayer closet, and one early spring afternoon I wandered out there just to rejoice in the Lord and to pray. I enjoyed the feel of the new boots on my feet, the first pair I had ever owned. Just a few days before, one of our young men—Chuck—had given them to me. He had been one of the toughest addicts who had ever come to Christian Farms. I've worn boots ever since.

I stood there on the knoll for a minute, stretching and feeling the good sun warm on my back and smelling the freshness of the air. I hadn't started to pray, so I wasn't particularly expecting the Lord to speak, but with no thought on my part, the sentence came.

"Look behind you."

I turned and looked back down at the farm. The buildings looked dressed up in their white and red coats of paint. I could see one of our young men driving Hope in from the pasture toward the red milking barn. Faith, our pregnant Black Angus beef cow, grazed nearby. Charity's piglets had grown up now and she was expecting a new litter any day. A dozen or more white chickens scratched in the yard or ambled around on the green grass.

It was exactly what the Lord had told me it would become before we left.

"Yes, Ben, it's time to move on."

21

"You're the Host!"

"MR. KINCHLOW?" THE VOICE on the telephone sounded businesslike, but friendly. "This is Ruth Eggert with CBN. I'm calling for Pat Robertson of the '700 Club.'"

My first thought was that this was probably a sales gimmick—a book club, an auto club, or something.

"What's the '700 Club'?" I asked.

The lady laughed politely and tried to explain. "the '700 Club' is a Christian talk show. It's broadcast over Channel 33 in Dallas every day, and we have guests come to the show to tell their testimony or talk about their ministries—anything unusual that the Lord may be doing in their lives."

She paused, and all I could think to say was, "Yes."

"We've been hearing about the ministry there in Killeen with drug addicts," she continued. "We'd like to have you come on the show and tell us about it."

I didn't have any idea what I was getting into, but it didn't take me two seconds to decide. "Lady, I'll go anywhere to talk about Jesus."

She set the time and the date and Vivian and I drove up to Dallas to be on this "700 Club."

We found Channel 33 in a not-so-new warehouse tucked away behind the Coca-Cola factory near Love Field in Dallas. The make-up lady powdered my nose and sat me down on the front row of the audience to wait my turn. A builder from Fort Worth and one other guest waited with me.

I was fascinated by the set, the lights, and the cameramen jockeying into position. A young man dashed around among the cameramen carrying sheets of paper and talking to first one and then the other. He was wearing earphones and had a little microphone hung around his neck.

Pretty soon the lights went down and the pace slowed. A rotund, jolly fellow walked out onto the set and settled into one of two chairs. A young lady started counting backward. When she got down to one, trumpets began playing and a taped orchestra let loose with "Heaven Came Down and Glory Filled My Soul." From somewhere off camera, an announcer opened the show. "Welcome to the '700 Club' with your co-host, Henry Harrison, and your host, Pat Robertson!"

Then while the music played and everybody clapped, this tall, pleasant-faced fellow with a shock of wavy hair came striding across the set, pulled out a chair, and sat behind a desk near Mr. Harrison. That had to be Pat Robertson.

I was glad they called the builder to come up first so I could get an idea of what to do. After his interview, the cameras shifted over to a bunch of people sitting at phones and talking to callers. A nice-looking fellow stood there and read into the camera from little sheets of paper what people all over Dallas were calling in about—answers to prayer, receiving Jesus as Savior, or being baptized in the Holy Spirit.

When I stepped on the set and eased into a chair next to Mr. Robertson, I felt pretty much at ease. I didn't have sense enough to be nervous. Pat was easy to talk to and started asking about my work with addicts. He seemed so interested that I really got into it. That led to talk about the past, and the change Jesus had made in my life, and I could always get excited about that.

I really enjoyed the show, and after it was over I met Don Hawkinson, the producer, and Jerry Bolin, the director. Vivian and I thanked the Lord all the way back to Christian Farms and talked about this television show that could get the word out about what He was doing all across the country. The lost were being saved, and people who had been Christians for years were being filled with the Spirit and revived. We were very excited over having seen it all, and to have shared in it, but that was it as far as we were concerned. Good-bye to the "700 Club" and Pat Robertson.

* * *

Life went on as usual at the farm, except that we knew our time there was short. I had already told Bob Bearden that I believed the Lord was getting ready to move me on to something else. But I wanted to stay on at the farm until the boys got out of school in the spring.

"Stay as long as you please, Ben," he said.

A couple of weeks went by, and one day the phone rang as it did so often. I assumed it would be another addict or alcoholic calling for help.

"Mr. Kinchlow," the friendly voice said, "this is CBN calling. We were wondering if you might fly to Portsmouth and help out with the '700 Club' next week. Of course, we'll pay your way."

That part sounded good. I figured they needed somebody to stand over by the telephones and read those little sheets of paper. I could handle that.

"Well, yes m'am, I think I can do that," I agreed.

In Portsmouth, Virginia, the entire set-up was impressive— from the two-story wall painting of Jesus in the lobby to the big studio with a balcony. This time I felt more like a veteran, so while the people with the cameras and microphones and sheets of paper scurried around, I found a place over by the telephones and had a good time talking to some of the counselors while we waited.

"Hi, there," I said to the guy on the front row. Then I shook hands with the lady next to him. "Pretty exciting, isn't it?" Then the gentleman next to her looked up and I felt as though I ought to shake hands with him, too. I was really having a good time meeting these people. They were polite and friendly and I was having a ball. One would have thought I was on the campaign trail.

The stage manager looked my way. "Sir, please take your place."

Well, I thought I *was* in my place! Now what? If I was

going to be on the show, the only other spot was the set. As usual, there was the host chair behind the desk and a place for the co-host and a guest to sit, so I figured the guest chair was for me. I dropped into it, wondering if they were going to have me tell my story all over again.

The stage manager turned around and saw me and looked startled. "Sir, we're ready to start the show. Please take your place."

It was two minutes to "Heaven Came Down," and I was wondering where all the hosts were. I shrugged and thought, "No skin off *my* nose." I looked back at the stage manager.

"Well, exactly where am I supposed to *be?*" I asked.

"You mean—nobody told you?"

"Told me *what?*"

"Pat's in Israel. You're the *host!*"

Before I had time to get scared, "Heaven Came Down" faded out and I was saying, "Welcome to the '700 Club.'"

* * *

That was my second appearance on television ever and I was the host—for two hours. I don't remember who the guests were, or what we talked about. I am certain I was awful, but our audience was small at the time and we probably had no way to handle complaints anyway.

However, CBN called again, and then again. And I went back to Portsmouth to host each time because Pat was doing a lot of traveling in those days. Soon I was invited to host two shows in Atlanta, and eventually I hosted for an entire week there.

And that was my introduction to the Christian Broadcasting Network and its flagship program, the "700 Club." It set in motion a chain of events that led to my employment as Counseling Director at the Network's Dallas station, to a move to the headquarters in Tidewater, Virginia, for a series of odd jobs, and eventually to my role as a regular co-host of the "700 Club" and a vice-president of the corporation. I have seen more than my share of miracles, but few exceeded the faithful provision and favor of God in setting me in the midst of one of the world's most unique ministries.

A seldom discussed aspect of this remarkable series of events was the courage, the daring, shown by Pat Robertson as president of the Christian Broadcasting Network as well as host of the "700 Club." This man, heading a fledgling organization based in the South, with stations in Atlanta, Dallas, and Portsmouth, Virginia—drawing a significant amount of his support from areas south of the Mason-Dixon line—did not hesitate to give a black man a central, visible role in his television operation. Indeed, his action preceded that of all the major television organizations. For this was long before the days of Ed Bradley on "Sixty Minutes," Max Robinson on ABC News, or Bryant Gumbel on "The Today Show."

Pat Robertson simply does not think in terms of skin color.

Why did God do what He's done?

The answer is quite simple and at the same time terribly profound: God has a plan for my life and for yours. And God's plan is *victory*. It will rule over every issue—race, background, fear, frustration, anger, and hatred if you will allow it. That plan may not include service in a worldwide ministry or national prominence. But it will ultimately include God's very best for you, along with eternal life, because it is built on a foundation of total and unconditional love. You see, God *loves* His creation, all of it—but more than that, God loves you and me, just the way we are. It's the hardest thing in the world for a man or woman, particularly for a black man or woman in America, a poor man or woman—the outcast, the suffering—to realize that the Creator of the universe loves us. But He does.

And He wants us to love Him, not because of some "ego stroke" or psychological quirk or need on His part, but because we were made for love and only He can satisfy the deep yearning in us all.

And even if we don't love Him, He still loves us. He made us as we are and He loves us as we are.

That fact—that objective, proven fact—provides the answer, the only permanent answer, to the question we glimpsed at the outset of this book: Will men ever be able to eliminate racial prejudice—white fearing and hating black, black hating and fearing white? Can India's caste system be overcome? Can South Africa's apartheid be solved? The answer to all these questions is a resounding yes. What we need is truth, not religion, but real truth. And truth is a person, and He has a name—Jesus Christ. We must accept and receive Him, freely, honestly, and openly, just the way we are now, and we must let Him work out reality for us and in us. A key point is that *we* must make the choice. Since we are made in God's image, we can make a choice, we can decide. That's a heavy truth. In all the creation, only man is given the freedom to make his own decisions. He can choose life—real life—or he can choose another path, which may seem good for a short while but will eventually lead to destruction. It's astounding that God would love us so much that He would make us in His likeness and give us the awesome freedom to choose. It is important to understand that. Every one of us is where we are today as a result of choice, a series of choices, or a lack of definite choice. Jesus said, "A man cannot have two masters. . . ." We must choose whom we will serve. Remember this: You become the slave of whatever choice you make and you can ultimately blame no one but yourself. You are the end product of your own choices.

In my case, I decided to do the things I did. No one forced me. I chose. God loved me enough to let me do that.

For the black man or the white man, the Mexican, the Indian, the Oriental, the following sentence is a significant piece of the reality that we are faced with: "There is neither Jew nor Greek, there is neither bond nor free, there is neither male nor female [nor black nor white nor brown nor yellow]: for ye are all one in Christ Jesus."[1]

We all stand equal in this unconditional, unchanging love. That simple, revolutionary truth has been hidden for centuries. It's been obscured by church doctrine, racism, theology, even evangelism. Most damaging, however, has been the perception of Christ by most people as the exclusive property of the Western white man. While they may hesitate to confess the suspicion openly, most minorities—American blacks in particular—perceive God and His Christ as white. Throughout recorded history, "the Christ" has been easily recognizable—long-haired, grave in demeanor, with downcast or sunken eyes, and invariably white—regardless of the culture or races hearing the gospel presentation. Too many of the presenters of the gospel either consciously or unconsciously perceive Christ as white. The result is a kind of condescending "preaching to the savage" as opposed to a true proclamation by an equal to an equal. The presenter generates a feeling, not of being a "debtor to all men," as Paul described himself, but of doing someone a favor. A certain arrogance prevails. Thus these "savages" become "converts," not "brothers in Christ."

The failure to perceive Christ as the Savior of *all* men, apart from cultural considerations or personal preconceptions, has prevented millions from seeing the truth as God has declared it. The simplest, greatest evangelistic tool has been the most neglected—love of the brethren. It is the one virtue no one can contradict. Real love is sought by all, and known by few. Once you grasp the truth of God's unconditional love, regardless of your station or lifestyle, you are free to accept yourself as you are and subsequently others as they are. The first great commandment, as described by Jesus, is "Thou shalt love the Lord thy God with all thy heart, and with all thy soul, and with all thy mind. The second is like unto it, He said: Thou shalt love thy neighbor as thyself."[2]

You see, God loves you. He knows all about you and expects you to love others as you love yourself. It's all right to have a healthy, positive feeling about the unique, special creation you are. Breathe deeply, revel in this truth: You are special, and God loves you—unreservedly, committedly, permanently. This is the basis for all hope.

Is there hope for all men everywhere? For you personally?

There is—for you and for all the world. My beautiful and wonderful wife, our three great sons, and I—all of us forgiven, healed, and whole—are living witnesses to that certainty. If He can bring order and purpose out of the chaos that was our lives, He can do it for anyone. He can do it for you.

Endnotes

Chapter 3

1. Proverbs 23:7.
2. Genesis 3:8–9.
3. Genesis 1:28, 31.
4. Genesis 2:18.
5. Genesis 2:21–25.
6. Genesis 3:8.
7. Genesis 3:7.
8. John 8:44.
9. Revelation 12:10.
10. Genesis 3:24.
11. Genesis 3:19.
12. Genesis 3:18.

Chapter 4

1. Romans 12:1–2.
2. John 8:31–32.
3. John 8:36.

Chapter 5

1. Hosea 4:6.
2. John 3:3.
3. Nehemiah 8:1.
4. Romans 10:13–17.
5. Romans 10:1–2.
6. Jeremiah 23:1–2.
7. Jeremiah 23:9–11.

Chapter 7

1. Galatians 5:22–23.
2. Galatians 5:24.
3. Galatians 5:25–26.
4. Matthew 7:24–25.
5. Galatians 3:26–29.

Chapter 10

1. James 1:14–15.

Chapter 12

1. Patrick Henry, speech in Virginia Convention, 23 March 1775.

Chapter 15

1. Galatians 6:2.
2. Matthew 23:27.

Chapter 17

1. Matthew 28:19.
2. John 17:21.
3. Luke 24:49.

Chapter 18

1. Hebrews 11:1.
2. Luke 4:12.
3. Romans 6:13.
4. Luke 22:26.
5. 1 Corinthians 6:17.
6. 2 Timothy 1:7.
7. Galatians 5:17.
8. Galatians 5:16.

Chapter 19

1. Matthew 18:20.

Chapter 21

1. Galatians 3:28.
2. Matthew 22:37–39.